The TOUCH of the Spirit

The TOUCH of the Spirit

Ralph W. Neighbour, Jr.

BROADMAN PRESS
Nashville, Tennessee

Unless otherwise indicated all Scripture quotations used in this book are from
The New English Bible © **The Delegates of the Oxford University Press and
The Syndics of the Cambridge University Press, 1961, 1970. Reprinted by permission.**

Dewey Decimal Classification Number 248.5
Library of Congress Catalog Card Number: 72-84243
Printed in the United States of America

This book is dedicated
to
The TOUCH Family

Preface

For too long we have tried our best to *do* something for our Lord, when all He has wanted was simply for us to be channels through which he might flow. We have overlooked this most important of all points. Clergymen have encouraged members who are spiritually bankrupt to share "an abundant life," seemingly unaware that *being* comes before *doing*. It is time for us to acknowledge that the training classes, programs, and strategies we have developed are worthless without Christ-filled lives. We first must know what it means to be so yielded to Christ that his life can simply *flow through us*. This important truth must overshadow everything else that occurs in our lives before we can become those who are able to "make disciples."

It is of utmost importance, I feel, that before *any* training is given for outreach there should first be a preceding period in which men and women are taught to understand the meaning of the Spirit-filled life. If this is not done, or if it is thought that anyone can use the TOUCH Ministries effectively without the Spirit-filled life, bitter disappointment will result! With that in mind, the material in Jack Taylor's "Prologue" is inserted as a "pre-conditioner" for the truths which follow.

These chapters have been written as the result of nearly thirteen years of experience in helping Christians share their faith. They contain simple lessons in areas often not understood by the laity.

With *only* outreach to the *Outsider* in mind, practical helps are provided in such mundane matters as how to use a small group, understanding communication patterns, and learning how to infiltrate the world of the unbeliever. Each of the "practical" chapters are there because thousands of Christians I have met needed instruction in these areas. However, this is *not* a "methods" book. The Holy Spirit can lead each man and woman into ministry if trusted to do so. If the lack of patterns for ministry seems frustrating, no apology is made!

Trying to footnote all of the material is an impossibility, mainly because of the assimilation of thoughts and concepts through the years. Since there is "nothing new under the sun," I gladly acknowledge those who have written before me in this field as contributing to these pages.

I am indebted to my dear friend, Miles Stanford, for assisting me to fully realize that God is Timeless, and He is never in a hurry when it comes to developing His children. He quotes Dr. A. H. Strong as saying, "When God wants to make an oak, He takes a hundred years, but when He wants to make a squash, He takes six months." The truths of the Spirit-filled life do not permeate a congregation quickly. Jack Taylor's dear flock did not see revival until after he preached for seven years on Deeper Life truths. Our "People Who Care" congregation (West Memorial Baptist Church) here in Houston is nearly three years old, and we are just now, as I write, beginning to experience a response in some hearts to the teaching of Spirit-filled living.

My greatest hesitancy in publishing this volume lies at this point. I would beg the reader to understand that TOUCH ministries are *not* for those who are carnally minded. Strong meat belongs to those who are mature, no longer satisfied with milk. We have been pre-conditioned by our religious culture to find "quickie solutions" to evangelism; a "Squash Church" will not be able to comprehend TOUCH!

I agree with a dear friend who responded to a reading of this manuscript by writing:

> Many will wholeheartedly enter into what you have set forth and experience results so far in advance of what they have known before that their service will be successful. And this is the very thing that blocks and replaces spiritual growth—their realization of need is crippled.

> Still others will grasp and use these carefully explained methods in a fleshly way, and, with sufficient personality and talent will outwardly go a long way. These will not have your personal leadership to prevent this.

> In order to avoid most all of this, the alternative is a reverse: as spiritual growth and preparation for service are doctrinally laid out step by step, the results for those who mean business will be the Lord Jesus reaching out through them in time; very few instructions, warnings, or exhortations will be necessary. The vine has the life and knows what it is doing—the abiding and growing branch will be fruitful with but a bit of careful trimming now and then.

The concepts of this book have actually been put into practice in many Southern Baptist churches. They were first tested at West Memorial Baptist Church in Houston. Then the *TOUCH Basic Training* workbook was produced and used in San Antonio at Castle Hills First Baptist Church. A further private publication of the workbook has now been tested by the Evangelism Research Foundation in churches in Virginia, North Carolina, South Carolina, Georgia, Illinois, and Texas, and it has been requested by missionaries on foreign mission fields. That which began as *theory* has been put into *practice.* The reader must understand as he reads the latter chapters that real, live people are really living in TOUCH with the "Outsiders" to be described.

A good "prequel" to this present book is Taylor's *The Key to*

Triumphant Living. One who leads will sense when others are ready for Spirit-controlled evangelism. When one drinks at this fountain, the taste of God's living waters spoils one forever; never again will "evangelism-made-easy" be appealing!

A special word of thanks is included for the willing hands of Gail Webb and Frances Berner for typing the manuscript and to Dr. David Haney and the Miles Stanfords for their brutal (and thus helpful!) critiques of the text.

For those who are ready, and for those who burn within with His love for the unreached, these pages are prayerfully provided for the glory of God.

RALPH W. NEIGHBOUR, JR.
Houston, Texas
1972

Contents

The
TOUCH
of the
Spirit

Prologue by Jack R. Taylor
How the Human Functions

Many believers are now limited in the matter of witnessing, especially in witnessing to the overcoming life, because they have not been taught to understand how the human functions. Passages of Scripture all through the Bible tell about a victorious, overcoming, and abundant life. In spite of them, for years I could not attest to them, because the Christian life I claimed to possess wasn't "overcoming" anything! When Christians get perfectly honest with themselves, the reason they don't witness is not because they don't know how, but because they do not have a relationship with the Indwelling Christ which has captured them, giving them an "overflow message." When you find Someone really worthwhile, Someone who captures your whole life, you are going to tell about Him! Of course, instructions are needed, but they will consist simply of suggestions about how to channel the overflow that comes from the Christ who dwells within.

If you have been doing a good work in your own strength, the work bears *your* mark. If Christ has been doing a good work through your life, it bears *the mark of the Lord.* There is a great deal of difference between a man doing his best for the Lord, and the Lord being allowed to do His normal work through that man. God's plan for you is for His life to be released *in* you so that the work you do bears more of the marks of the likeness of God than it does the image of man.

For a number of years all the spiritual excitement I had was what I could muster up as I sought to perform the work of the Lord. Things became so dull that one day I decided I would just quit if there couldn't be more! *There just happened to be more,* and that's why I'm writing this prologue. When Jesus commissioned the disciples, he gave them directions. He gave them the mandate to preach, and then in Luke 24:49 he said: "And mark this: I am sending upon you my Father's promised gift; so stay here in this city until you are armed with the power from above." In Acts 1:8 the last thing He said was this: "But you will receive power when the Holy Spirit comes upon you; and you will bear witness for me in Jerusalem, and all over Judaea and Samaria, and away to the ends of the earth."

We are kidding ourselves today if we pretend to witness before we know with assurance what this "power from on high" is. We cannot witness until we possess a proper relationship to the Holy Spirit—a relationship in which we receive his fulness. Through the use of three illustrations, it will become clear that it is not an *option,* but an *absolute necessity* for everyone who supposes to serve the Lord *to be filled with the Holy Spirit, absolutely controlled by the Lord.*

The text for our study is found in 1 Thessalonians 5:23. This Scripture tells us that man is made up of three basic parts: "May God himself, the God of peace, make you holy in every part, and keep you sound in spirit, soul, and body, without fault when our Lord Jesus Christ comes. He who calls you is to be trusted; he will do it."

Consider first man's component parts: he has a body, a soul, and a spirit.

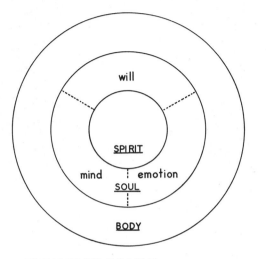

THE NATURE OF MAN

Fig. 1

The *spirit* is the inner man, designed to be the dwelling place of God, from which He controls the entirety of a man's personality.

The *soul,* if it could be subdivided, would be separated into *mind, will,* and *emotions.* Within the soul of man, all the decision-making processes occur. The interaction of mind, will, and emotions cannot be separated; all participate in the thinking, emoting, and deciding actions.

The *body* is the house in which soul and spirit abide.

From this basic diagram of man, Paul tells us, in Corinthians, that there are three kinds of people. He describes *the natural man, the carnal man,* and *the spiritual man.*

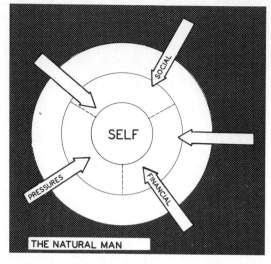

Fig. 2

The Bible describes the natural man as being "dead" (Eph. 2:1). He is not dead in his personality; he is as alive there as is the Christian. He also has a body, very much alive. His "deadness" is in the *spirit.*

Note that the division between "soul" and "spirit" could almost be eliminated; in the natural man, the life of the spirit is inoperative. The natural man is under the control of the "self," the "I." The devil has great power in this man's world and is forever exerting external pressures upon this man. He is literally in the devil's domain.

The devil is the god of this world (2 Cor. 4:4). Men and women in Christian service have all too completely disregarded the work of the devil. Whether a believer is TOUCHing Outsiders or simply going out to visit for the church, when he gets into the matter of witnessing and winning, *he has entered into the domain of the devil,* and he can expect Satan to counterattack!

Further, the devil is very much afraid of a Christian becoming Spirit-filled because he knows such a Christian will discover secrets which Satan has tried to keep concealed for centuries. One of them is that *HE IS*. Teen-agers have a song that says, "Everybody ought to know who Jesus is." We ought to have another one: "Everybody ought to know who Satan is." The more Jesus takes control of a life, the more active Satan will become.

Since the natural man lives only in Satan's world, he has no inner resistance to Satan except the "I" which lives in his spirit. God does not control his life; indeed, *God is not in his life!* The natural man is a fallen creature, and he finds his life shaped by expediencies and circumstances. No wonder he is "shaped in the fashion of this world," for the devil enters him at will, freely influencing his mind, his will, and his emotions.

The devil has no problem controlling such an individual; he can do it in several different ways. A person does not have to be possessed by the devil to be controlled by him, for the natural man's world contains multiple circumstances which the devil can manipulate to control him indirectly. He is a natural man: with emotions no stronger than he has, with a will no stronger than he has, with a mind no stronger than he possesses, he is absolutely no match for the devil. The devil uses financial, social, and educational pressures to absolutely control his life.

All Christians ought to realize that when they go out to witness to a man who is lost, they are dealing with a man who is held in the snare of Satan! When the Christian reaches out to the unbeliever, he is entering the devil's domain. He is reaching out to one who is not only egocentric, but who in reality is controlled by the devil who invades him at his will. The natural man is dead to God's inner presence. This man has a "God-shaped vacuum" in his life: he is dead in his spirit, which was made to be inhabited by God. His "soul" is in control. The natural man lives in his soul; he lives only in the characteristics of his mind, will, and emotions. He has never become alive with God in his spirit; there, he is a dead man.

He is a dead man when it comes to God! The things of God mean nothing to him. He cannot even be condemned by the Christian for not having an appetite for spiritual things. He is as dead to spiritual things as bodies in the graveyard are dead to physical things. The Bible says he does not perceive the matters of the Spirit: they are mysteries to him (1 Cor. 2:14). He doesn't know a thing about godly control.

It is no small matter for Christians to reach unbelievers for Jesus Christ. If Christians are taught that all one must do is memorize the "Roman Road," or memorize a specific "plan of salvation," and then go out and try to convince a natural man to become a Christian, they will find that they will fail miserably. Only God can break through the barriers in the way!

Fig. 3

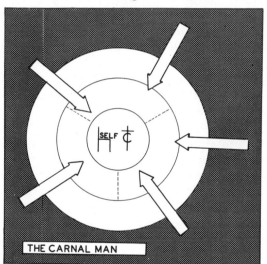

The carnal man is an unyielded Christian. Somewhere in the past, his mind, will, and emotions were invaded by a witness for Christ. Perhaps a Christian was used by the Holy Spirit to neutralize the power of Satan; at some point in his life, he has heard about Jesus. His hungry mind and hungry emotions responded, and he received Jesus Christ into his life. He has made the most critical decision a man ever makes, and he has now entered the most critical time of his entire life as a new Christian.

He has two avenues before him: first, he may move into a relationship with his Savior in which Christ is given the right to "mind his own business" within him. Second, he may choose to control his own life, deliberately refusing to give Christ "throne rights." If this happens, he is a carnal Christian. He has received Christ into his spirit, but refuses to permit him to become the "resident boss" of his soul and his body.

Undoubtedly, the carnal man joins a church. Let's just say he joins a Baptist church. I pray he will get more instruction than I did! I was given the "typical" set of instructions twenty-seven years ago when I joined a Baptist church . . . when I went forward, somebody told me to sit down, and that was all the instruction I ever received!

I obeyed completely. I "sat down," *but then came the hunger.* The deep joy which entered my life when I was born again lasted several weeks, but I soon found that when I tried to face problems in my own strength, I was as weak as I had been as an unbeliever. Early in my Christian life I began to suspect that there *had to be something more than this to being a Christian.* I knew Christ had come into my life; I had asked him to. He was *in* my life, but because no one told me what the "more" was, I was still in control of my life. The devil could still reach into me through outward circumstances; I just didn't have much victory!

Does the devil stop his attacks when a man gets saved? Does he give up on a baby Christian? Absolutely not! If anything, he multiplies his attack. He doesn't like what has happened; if he can discredit the "good news" contained in a person's salvation, cause him to be disenchanted with his relationship to Christ and His church, the devil will gladly oblige. The devil continues to attack!

The carnal person finds himself continually attacked by the devil. He fights a defending battle against these attacks, but he is inconsistent. The Bible describes the carnal Christian as one who is infantile, who responds as a baby in times of need. As a baby, he cannot tell where his own life ends and the life of his world begins; he is closely intertwined with his environment. He is not spiritually mature. Go through all the qualities of a little baby, and you will describe how many, many church members act spiritually. For example, when a baby does not get his way, he cries. When he gets hungry or doesn't understand, he cries. When something doesn't go his way, he throws a tantrum. We've got enough carnal Christians in our churches today to understand how a Christian "baby" functions. They have to be fed with milk and not with meat (1 Cor. 3:1-4). They can't understand the deep things of the Lord. When something comes along that they can't understand, they are prone to get upset about it.

Paul's prayer for the carnal man in 1 Thessalonians 5:23 is that he might be wholly cleansed . . . completely cleansed . . . and sanctified! He prays for two things: first, for *cleansing;* second, after being cleansed, he prays the carnal man will be *filled and preserved in a state of being God-controlled.*

The carnal person is not so! Worries come, and anxieties come. From the outside world, the domain of the devil, he finds himself constantly being bent out of shape by the world. As with the natural man, expediencies in his world shape this man. Christ is *in* his life, but Christ is not *controlling* his life. Because Christ is resident, however, sometimes this man is more miserable than the natural man, for in the natural man there is not much of a struggle. The devil controls him without any resistance, but in the life of the carnal man, there is the frustrating knowledge that Christ lives within and that He is not pleased with the life being lived. The carnal man ranges between guilt and pleasure, between self-loathing and self-loving, wanting to do good—but evil is always active in him. Chapter 7 in the book of Romans is a picture of the carnal man wrestling with his carnal self.

The spiritual man has chosen God's will in the place of his own will for every situation, for the rest of his life. He has acknowledged that the only purpose for his existence is to be a container for the Holy Spirit. The Spirit of God is to have full control over his soul, with its intellect, emotions, and will, and over his body.

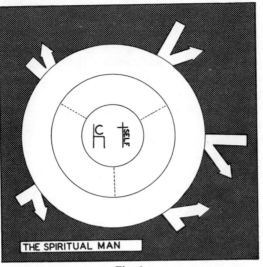

THE SPIRITUAL MAN

Fig. 4

He accepts his role as simply being a "temple for the Holy Spirit." He has settled the fact that he is "not his own."

There is as much difference between the spiritual and carnal man as there is between the carnal and natural man. In fact, the carnal and natural man are sometimes very difficult to tell apart. You can stand them up beside each other, and they will act pretty much the same. Both are rather sensitive to the things of the world and insensitive to the things of God. Both of them have their ego, their self-will, in control. Both of them find themselves greatly affected by outward circumstances. The majority of the people whom we call "Christians" would fall somewhere in the category of being carnal. They live with all interests turned outside, into their world. They have not found victory over their world.

Every man needs to be filled with the Spirit. As further chapters will affirm, "TOUCH" training is merely *the implementation of what is to be done through men whose lives have been opened to the eternal resources of the Lord Jesus Christ.*

There are a few basic things a Christian must do to be filled:

One, *he must be cleansed.* That is, he must confess every sin in his past, bringing his confession of sins up to date, and have those sins forgiven (1 John 1:9).

Two, *he must choose against himself.* That is what Jesus meant when he said, "If anyone wishes to be a follower of mine, he must leave self behind; day after day he must take up his cross, and come with me" (Luke 9:23)—choose against himself.

Three, *he must choose death to himself.* He reckons for himself what God has already reckoned.[1]

Four, *he must choose the will of God deliberately.* He must be ready to begin praying, "Lord, I choose your will in the place of my will in every situation, *for the rest of my life."* Then Jesus is crowned Lord. When these things happen in the life, one may be absolutely certain that God will respond by filling him with the Spirit.

The greatest need today in our churches is to settle this matter of being properly related to the Holy Spirit! There is so much confusion about what it means to be filled with the Spirit; it is crucial to settle on the fact that God the Spirit already lives inside of every person who is a Christian. Further, the Holy Spirit is ready to *fill* every Christian. When we meet His conditions, He begins to fill us. He simply needs a yielded life in order to turn the carnal man into the spiritual man.

One of the greatest thrills a pastor can have, as thrilling as leading a natural man to become a Christian, is to show a carnal man who has been a Christian for many years how to become Spirit-filled. Not long ago a woman came to my office. She had been reading a little leaflet which explained the Spirit-filled life. She was troubled, for some of her friends were going to extremes in Pentecostalism. I shared the good news of the Christ-owned life with her, and she found the victorious life right then for herself! She is typical of thousands of other Christians in churches across our land who are *starving to death spiritually,* all the while wanting to know how to find the victorious life in Jesus Christ!

The basic difference between the carnal and spiritual person is determined by who is in control. Mark well this fact: the Spiritual man is not one who "tries to be spiritual." No one can live the Christian life but Christ himself. Only when he is "resident boss" within the life is one a spiritual man.

Too often sermons leave people with the impression that if they would just strike a pose of looking uncomfortable and miserable, they would be "spiritual" and have a "holy" look. There exists today a brand of Christians who seem to believe they are "holy" if they can sit down and look uncomfortable. They seem to say, "I'd rather be a Christian than be happy." We should not wonder why people do not go for a faith like that! Being holy is not striking a pose about halfway between a migraine headache and acid indigestion.

SELF, OR RIVERS OF LIVING WATER?

What is the fruit of the Spirit? The Scripture says the first fruit is *love,* the next one *joy,* the next one *peace.* And we could go on, describing nine exciting qualities. Jesus said in John 7:38, " 'If anyone is thirsty let him come to me; whoever believes in me, let him drink.' As Scripture says, 'Streams [rivers] of living water should flow out from within him.' " Notice . . . rivers of love, rivers of joy, rivers of peace flow from the man filled with the Spirit. These are the qualities God desires every Christian to possess.

The spiritual man has come to the end of self-owned living. He has decided that self (ego) does not deserve to run his life, and that self is the greatest problem in his life. Further, not only has he decided that self does not need to run his life, but that *self needs to be assigned to the place God himself has assigned it.* At our invitation, Jesus Christ will come to sit on the throne of our life. What, at that time, are we going to do with self? It is going to go where it belongs—*to the cross.*

We must frankly admit we don't understand all Paul meant when he talked about "self being crucified," but *he did mean everything he said!* When he said, "Reckon ye yourselves to be dead unto sin," that's what he meant! When he said, "Don't you know that when you were baptized into Christ you were baptized into His death?" he meant it! He was not speaking of water baptism; he referred to Spirit baptism, by which the Holy Spirit immerses us into the person of Christ, until both of us are one. When we became a Christian, we were baptized into Christ by the Holy Spirit; at that time, God reckoned everything to us that He had reckoned to Jesus Christ.

Did Jesus Christ die for our sins? Then we died *with Him* for our sins. I cannot fully understand the doctrine of co-crucifixion, but I know if God decreed it, I had better agree with it, whether I understand it or not. Two vital things happened at Calvary: first, Jesus died for me. That settled my *sin-guilt* problem. Second, I died with Him. That settled my *sin-self* problem. I am to "reckon" it (count on it as a continuing fact) to be so. If I don't reckon that I died with Him, I'll not have settled my sin-self problem.

A great many people have settled the sin-guilt problem in their hearts and know they are going to heaven, but as Bertha Smith has said, "There are many people who are going to heaven who are having a hell of a time of it!" *This is true simply because they have not found the secret of overcoming in the matter of self.*

What should the Christian do with self? Some say, "Let's discipline it. Let's send it to school." Some even send self to college and to seminary, and require self to take all the study courses; all that is accomplished is the development of a well-trained, well-disciplined self. (Sometimes this becomes the most dangerous expression of it!) Others say, "Let's domesticate it. Let's train it. Self is like a wild animal. Let's tame it down." When they finish, they still have self, now both disciplined and domesticated.

Of course, the most religious thing you can do with self is "dedicate" it or "rededicate" it. Some say, "Lord, I'll tell you what I'm going to do: I'm going to employ my full self for you. Lucky, lucky you! You are going to have advantage of all my self."

God does not want a gift of your self-life. He dealt with self by crucifying it on the cross, but we've still got acres and acres of dedicated self in our churches. In times of difficulty and times of pressure, you can always tell whether self is dead. When it is not, it will erupt like a volcano! What does God want us to do with it? We are to reckon it where God has already reckoned it, and that is *dead!*

Someone says, "Wait a minute. I 'reckoned' that to be so, but my *self* comes alive again so easily. Why?" Remember—it is a *reckoned* death. You are not dead, and sin is not dead. You have simply reckoned that the dominion, the reign of sin-self has ended. Jesus has entered your life to introduce another nature inside your life, and that's "The Jesus Nature." The Spirit-filled life is simply Jesus, minding his own business in you.

JESUS HAS THE PROBLEMS IN THE SPIRIT-FILLED MAN

Does the devil stop working on a man when he decides that Jesus may have the controls of his life? Absolutely not! The newly yielded man will have more problems than he has ever had before—or will he? Do dead men have problems? *All the problems will belong to Jesus;* when a man has settled the fact that he is "no longer his own," he has no problems. Even self, the greatest problem, belongs to Jesus. Here is what happens to a person who turns to Jesus, who absolutely allows Jesus to be his Lord: he sees a flock of problems coming and he says, "Jesus, here they come. I thank you that I don't have to be related to them, except as you choose to be related *in me* to them. Jesus, here are your problems. What are you going to do? Live out your solution through my body and soul."

The Spirit-filled Christian does not have to worry about anything but being properly related to Christ, who in turn chooses to relate him to all difficulties as He chooses to be related to them, and that is victory. For too long, too many Christians have been directly related to too many problems. I don't know about you, but I've never handled one properly in my entire life. It doesn't take a genius, then, to discover whom we ought to trust. I've never succeeded, and He has never failed. Ought we not, then, to be able to absolutely trust Him?

Without question, the devil's onslaughts continue—but what has happened? The power of God has become an inner source of strength within the Spirit-filled life. Down in the *spirit,* where man was made to contain God, something has happened. Jesus Christ has taken control.

What about the *soul,* comprised of the mind, the will, the emotions? Does the Spirit-filled personality change because Jesus takes over? There will slowly be a personality change, but I am still the individual He redeemed. I keep the basic personality He meant for me to have when He created me, but now there begins what the Bible calls "sanctification." Sanctification is simply the life "being cleansed, being set apart." The power of Jesus Christ begins to emanate from the inner man, the spirit, to take over the will, to capture the mind, to capture the emotions. When Jesus takes over, impulses to worry still come to the emotions; the stresses that would overwhelm the will still come; the doubts that would flood the mind still come . . . but Jesus Christ has filled the emotions, the will, the mind, and these are now "set apart" for Him to control.

All of our problems as carnal Christians come because we have nothing but self in the rooms of our life. Why do men worry? Self! Why do men get angry? Self! Why do we get frustrated? Self! When you deal with self, allowing Jesus to be "resident boss," He is at the receiving end of all the problems: they go to Him. "It is God who works in us, both to *will* and to *do* His good pleasure." "Let this mind, the mind of Christ, be in you."

Do you have trouble handling emotions? I do. For years, I tried to love and I could not. I tried to have that Scripture-promised peace and joy; I tried to tell myself by means of "the power of positive thinking" that all would be well. It did not work! Enthroned self had no answer to my dilemma.

When Jesus Christ fills us, He takes the body, the agency of contact with the outside world, and He begins to express Himself through it. Evangelism thus becomes all of Him, and none of self.

Jesus promised, "If anyone is thirsty, let him come to me . . . and drink." The Scripture says, "He that believes, out of *HIS INNER MAN* will flow rivers of living water" (John 7:38-39, KJV). Notice: Jesus Christ is the source of all this, living inside my body. He has broken into my mind, emotions, will, and now He controls me.

My will is His. He has dealt with self; self stays on the cross as I continue to reckon it so, and Jesus stays on the throne. As

He does, having previously lacked for love, I become a river of love. I, who couldn't even have enough self-confidence to have peace within my life, now find a river of peace flowing from within. It goes on and on: joy, kindness, goodness, on and on! THIS INITIATES SPIRIT-FILLED EVANGELISM!

JACK R. TAYLOR

NOTES

1. For a more complete treatment of this subject, see *The Key to Triumphant Living* (Nashville: Broadman Press, 1971).

Chapter 1
The Lion Got Peanuts

The story is told about the small-town zoo that bought a young, vigorous lion. They caged him with an older one who had tired claws and retired vocal cords. The old lion would sleep in the back of the cage until mealtime while the young lion roared and leaped continually at the bars of the cage to entertain the onlookers.

When mealtime came, the older lion got huge chunks of red meat. The young lion got peanuts.

He got weaker and weaker. Finally he said to the sleepy senior in the shade, "What gives? I work my tail into curlycues entertaining the people, and I get peanuts; you sleep and get meat!"

Said the old Leo, "Well, you see, this is a small-town zoo, and they have a limited budget. To get past the City Council, they booked you in here as a monkey." [1]

To many, that story is not a funny joke. It is a pathetic parable. The old lion represents a senior clergy which has accepted its role as "Holy Men" in the life of the church, and the young lion suggests a confused laity which is continually being asked to do the "busy-work" required to keep the church cranked up.

It is totally untrue that preachers are supposed to "minister" while the laity becomes a "support system" for them! Yet, Mrs. Brown will usually introduce her pastor as "The Minister." She considers herself far below him in spiritual depth and not at all as one expected to minister in her world.

Moreover, many of the laity like it that way. I still remember the huffy church member who refused to share Christ because "they pay preachers to do that!"

Take the word "layman," for example. Ask a physician what a "layman" is, and he would probably say, "An amateur in medicine—someone who is a nonprofessional." Even so, the church member considers himself a nonprofessional. He is made to think that, because he does not have ordination, he is a spiritual amateur who is incapable of being a minister.

The English word "clergyman" comes from the Greek *klaros,* which refers to one chosen by the casting of a lot. The *klaros* was chosen by God to proclaim, to teach, to preach. The word "laity" comes from the Greek *laos,* meaning "people of God." All "people of God" are called to ministry, not just the clergymen. Anyone who is a member of the laity is a minister; the clergyman, in addition to his called-out tasks of preaching and teaching, is also a minister. *Anyone who is a Christian is a minister.*

This tragic distinction has distorted our concept of evangelism beyond biblical recognition. How can we break with this error? How did we end up with a cluster of professional clergymen controlling the Christian community, manipulating denominational structures, encouraging the laity to stand back and watch them minister?

Christians talk about renewing the church, about renewing the methodology of the structures, but before we can have the proper methods, we must have a proper theology! *Theology breeds methodology.*

Over two years ago I resigned from a denominational position. I left the most wonderful group of men with whom I have ever worked and the most pleasant task I have ever had. I accepted the questionable opportunity of pastoring a Houston church-without-walls, committed to be a parable among sister churches, a "guinea pig" for research and development of tomorrow's church structure. Some of my closest friends wondered if I had lost my senses.

Our little flock of thirty-two was determined that we would structure our lives to focus upon evangelizing the unchurched and redesigning yesterday's methods to find God's blueprint for tomorrow's church. *The longer we shared our common life, the more obvious it became that methods always come out of theology.*

When I came to Houston, I told my pastor friends, "My theology will not change, only my methods." How wrong I was! Our theology has been continually tested by the power of Scripture, changing radically from a theology of *klaros* ministry. We have realized that *every child of God is a minister of God.*

That revolutionary truth was only the beginning. The Word taught us that the phrase "being saved" was misunderstood by many. The question was asked, "What are we saved *from?*" The answer frequently was, "We are saved *from* hell and *for* heaven."

Not so! Salvation involves being removed from a life of SIN. To understand that, remove the "S" and "N" from the word and place the "I" on the throne of the life. We are saved from an "I-life," self-regulated and self-controlled. If this "I" is dethroned, the obvious consequence of salvation is the immediate transfer of control of life to Jesus Christ. We, then, are no longer our own . . . we are temples, to be indwelled by the Christ who becomes resident boss in our lives.

If I am "saved," I shall live in the will of Christ. Since he is not willing for any to perish, it is obvious his inner lordship of my life will propel me into *ministry.* We are all ministers.

Unfortunately, this truth is not taught from all pulpits. Often the emphasis is, "Accept Jesus as your Savior. Be sure that if you die tonight you will not go to hell." A child or adult says to himself, "I don't want to die and fry! I'll 'get saved' right now." He walks the aisle, shakes the preacher's hand, perhaps someone prays; he is voted into the church and is then baptized.

The result of this will be an "Instant Carnal Christian." How can such a new Christian be anything *but* carnal? The preacher promised him a happy after-life, but said nothing about the lordship of Christ. Born carnal, the new Christian settles back to keep his Life Assurance policy paid up by tithing, attending, and working hard in the organizations . . . and retains full control of his own life!

We are trapped in a deadly cycle of carnal evangelism. The preacher offers other-worldly salvation, producing carnal Christians who fill pews. Since they are not yielded, they let the preacher "minister." Carnal Christians know full well they have no witness to bear. They can be sent through all the "lay evangelism" courses we can crank out, but the best response we can expect will be carnal Christians working apart from the Spirit at an impossible task.

If a man believes in Jesus because he wants to go to heaven when he dies, what does he do about *ministry?* He hires a "Holy Man." If the Holy Man needs help, the laymen hire an "Assistant Holy Man." They are told, "Holy men, you make your living by evangelizing. Do your thing! Be Holy. We laymen may cuss or have a beer, but if you do that, you aren't Holy. Don't do what we do."

The Holy Man gets caught up in the System; what is he to do, with kids to support? How does he prove he is a Holy Man? Why, ask any layman on any pulpit committee. The holiest Holy Men can be discovered by examining the associational minutes. You will know them by their baptismal records and their increases in Sunday School.[2]

If the Holy Man is ambitious, if he wants to be called to the "Big Church,"[3] he has to persuade more and more people to "believe in Jesus and go to heaven." (Believe me, your baptisms really drop when you begin to explain that personal commitment to Christ will literally cost one his life!) So he preaches his "Easy Believism," producing more and more carnal Christians . . . who get elected to pulpit committees, etc.

Where will this end? It will go on and on, sucking the life out of us, until the laity rebel against the whole mess, demanding the proclamation of an adequate theology of redemption that can change it all. It will go on until they require the Star Quarterback Holy Men to get over on the sidelines and become the Humble Coach Servants, equipping every man, woman, and child to be a minister. It will go on until Spirit-filled evangelism becomes the only spiritually and socially acceptable kind within the life of the church.

Spirit-filled evangelism is evangelism which does not manipulate people, which declares the full message of salvation, and which never says less than: "Mister, if you would be a follower of Jesus Christ, you must be willing to turn the control of your life from self to the Savior, who wishes to take you out of your self-owned condition. When He enters your life, you will find yourself in the continual process of dying; every day you live you will die to self, living only to be His holy temple. You will bear within yourself the death of Jesus Christ and the life of God."

That is Spirit-filled evangelism! *It will require a major revolution in the church.* It will require that kind of revolution where the evangelist recognizes the fact that he is powerless unless he preaches with proper theology, regardless of the resulting statistics. It will require the kind of evangelism where every member of the *laos* quit hiring Holy Men to do their work for them and begin to do it themselves!

Spirit-filled evangelism happened one week in Houston, Texas, when a minister of West Memorial walked down the street and spent two hours talking to a mother who is far from God. That minister is a *woman Baptist!* Can you imagine a woman Baptist being a minister? Ministry took place when Linda went over to the nearby apartment and led Hazel to Christ. Ministry happens every time the people of God simply reveal their indwelling Christ!

NOTES

1. Thanks to my Methodist friend, Rev. Ed Beck of Denver, Colorado, for the inspiration for this chapter.

2. A leading denominational official told me recently, "When pulpit committees come to me for recommendations, they want to know two things, in the following order of importance: (1) How many did the preacher baptize last year? and (2) How fast is his Sunday School growing?" He cautioned me that West Memorial would never be respected by others until we showed ourselves adequate in these two areas!

3. *Ibid.*

Chapter 2
Spirit-Filled Evangelism

Then one of the seraphim flew to me carrying in his hand a glowing coal which he had taken from the altar with a pair of tongs. He touched my mouth with it and said,
> See, this has touched your lips;
> your iniquity is removed,
> and your sin is wiped away.

Then I heard the Lord saying, Whom shall I send? Who will go for me? And I answered, Here am I; send me. He said, Go and tell this people . . . (Isa. 6:6-9).

There is a great deal of confusion in Christendom today about the Holy Spirit. To some, the Holy Spirit is an "It," a Power, an impersonal "Something" within the universe. This is basically an Eastern concept: the Holy Spirit seems to become the "Yang" of the Yin and Yang.

Today's Christianity also contains another group who seem to believe that the Holy Spirit is basically an *experience*. Even as one experiences plunging into water, so one experiences the "baptism of the Holy Spirit." They teach that the Holy Spirit is available only *after* we have received Jesus Christ, as a "second work of grace." At a later date than conversion, one receives the Holy Spirit as an experience, often involving speaking in tongues.

Both of these groups shortchange themselves because they miss a greater truth.

WHO IS THE HOLY SPIRIT?

In this brilliant and majestic style, Paul presents one of the most important clues concerning the Godhead to be found anywhere in the Bible in Romans 8:9-17. Beginning in verse 9, Paul uses these phrases interchangeably: "God's Spirit," "the Spirit of Christ," "Christ dwelling within you," "the Spirit is life," "the Spirit of him who raised Jesus from the dead," "the God who raised Christ Jesus from the dead," "His indwelling Spirit," "by the Spirit," "the Spirit of God," "the Spirit you have received," "a Spirit that makes us sons," "and the Spirit of God joins with our spirit."

Don't miss the fact that Paul uses the above phrases interchangeably! He is making it very, very clear that *the Holy Spirit is God.* To Paul, God the Father, God the Son, and God the Holy Spirit are the same. The Spirit of God is in Christ; the Holy Spirit is in the Father; the Father is in the Holy Spirit.

Moreover, Paul sees the Spirit of God as resident in all of creation and always, always, always resident in every Christian—from the moment he becomes a child of God! One does not "receive Jesus Christ" and later on receive the "baptism of the Holy Spirit." This is both a doctrinal and experiential error. When a seeker receives Jesus, he receives all there is of God!

Who is the Holy Spirit? [1] Jesus made an ultimate statement when He said, "God is Spirit." What did He mean?

In 1 Corinthians 2:10 we read, "For the Spirit explores everything, even the depths of God's own nature." As an illustration of that, Paul continues, "Among men, who knows what a man is but the man's own spirit within him?"

What is Paul saying here? Let me illustrate. I am named Ralph Neighbour. My friends know the spirit of Ralph Neighbour because he lives in a body. Within that body there are a mind, emotions, and a will. As my mind, emotions, and will inhabit this body, they are intimately, continuously related to it. They comprise my soul. Through my soul, housed or cased inside my body, I am constantly revealing to you a spirit that lives inside body and soul. We call this entity "Ralph Neighbour." I am more than my intellect, my will, my emotions, and my body; I am a "spirit," living within them. Ralph Neighbour is essentially a spirit. "Who knows what a man is, but the man's own spirit within him?"

One of these days this body will rot. This mind may decay through a process of aging. It may even become senile and unable to remember things. Perhaps one day my emotions may be destroyed by the stress of life. They may break down, be unable to function adequately or properly. One day my will might crack, might disintegrate . . . but the spirit of Ralph Neighbour will go on living. My body may die, but my spirit will live on eternally. Ralph Neighbour is a spirit, revealing himself through his body, his mind, his emotions, and his will.

My friends say they "know me," but all they really know are the expressions of me which emanate from my body and soul.

The Scriptures tell us that God, too, is a Spirit. Consider two parallel descriptive phrases for the word "spirit." The first one is the "inner self." Who knows Ralph Neighbour fully except the "inner self" that is within him? Another parallel phrase used to describe "spirit" is "the within one." Who knows the "spirit" of Ralph Neighbour but "the within one" in him? I am an "inner self," a "within one," a "spirit," living behind my body, intellect, emotions, and will.

God is also Spirit. He is Inner Self. He is The Within One. Paul continues, "In the same way, only the Spirit of God knows what God is. This is the Spirit that we have received from God, and not the spirit of the world, so that we may know all that God of his own grace has given us. . ."

I have a spirit, and I reside in a form which makes it possible for me to express the spirit of Ralph Neighbour. So it is with God. He is The Holy Spirit. He is The Inner Self. He is the one Real Person, the one Inner Self, the Complete Within One in all of the universe. As a Spirit He is invisible, unapproachable, and unreachable except to Himself.

How can we know God? He is a Spirit. Does He have a form, a shape, through which He expresses Himself? The Scripture teaches that the Spirit of God, the Within One, needed something encapsuled around Him in order that He might reveal Himself. God has arranged to reveal Himself by being inside His creation. The Scripture tells us in Genesis that the Spirit, the Within One, "moved upon the face of the waters" (Gen. 1:2, KJV). God has revealed Himself in what He has created.

In Romans 1:20, Paul explains "His invisible attributes, that is to say his everlasting power and deity, have been visible, ever since the world began, to the eye of reason, in the things he has made." When man looks at creation, he sees God within it. If man wants to know how great God is, he may look at the galaxies of stars. God is within them, revealing to all mankind how great and grand and massive He is. Man looks at the atom, and in it sees His preciseness, His consummate regard for detail, and above all His knowledge which is beyond understanding. God tells mankind something about Himself through every wild flower in the forest, revealing that the Within One loves beauty.

In fact, whenever man looks at what God has made, he discovers God within, revealing something of Himself through all creation. The preacher states in Acts 14:17, " he has not left you without some clue to his nature, in the kindness he shows: he sends you rain from heaven and crops in their seasons, and gives you food and good cheer in plenty." God is constantly in the process of revealing all He is through all He has made.

A carpenter makes a grandfather clock. When he finishes it, it is separate from him. That is, his "spirit" does not live in the clock. The carpenter is here; the grandfather clock is there. However, when God makes a universe, a tree, a forest, a stream, He can reveal Himself through them. He is, of course, far more than what He creates, even as the spirit of a human is more than body, mind, and emotions.

In the same way my body is "me" and yet I am more than

my body, so God is in the atom, color, music, the rain that falls, the crops that grow . . . yet He is more than these things. He is the Spirit, the Inner Self, the Within One in all of creation—yet unfathomably more than it all.

Norman Grubb says this thought is "the key to all truth": *everything God created has been made essentially for one purpose, and that is to reveal Himself.* Everything we see has been made in order that we might know something more about God. When we see the Grand Canyon or the stars, we see the evidence of God. Everything we see—including you—has been made in order that the One Spirit, the One Inner Self, the One Person who is the creator of this universe might reveal something of Himself through what He has made.

Most important of all, God provided a complete revelation of Himself by placing His own fullness—"the fullness of the Godhead"—bodily within Jesus Christ. Humanity was presented with One who was totally, completely human, yet contained within Himself the full, complete Spirit of God. Jesus Christ revealed those qualities of God that nature could never reveal—redemptive love, justice, righteousness, tenderness, and a thousand other characteristics. *All that could possibly be known of God was encapsuled within Christ Jesus. The revelation of God was complete. Both Creation and the Son were "witnesses" to Him.*

The extent of the divine revelation embodied in Jesus Christ was *total* and *complete*! John declared that the Word had existed *"when all things began,"* and that this Word was *"what God was."* Further, it was through this same Word that *"all things came to be,"* and *"all that came to be was alive with his life."* That very same Word who had already revealed Himself partially as The Within One of the universe now came to men embodied in Jesus Christ of Nazareth, to be *"the light of men"* (John 1:John 1:1-4). He was, indeed, *"the offspring of God himself,"* *"become flesh to dwell among men."* Finally, through the son of a Jewish maiden, the Within One would reveal His glory, *"such glory as befits the Father's only Son, full of grace and truth"* (John 1:14).

In this divine creation of revelation, all that could or would be known of God has been fully expressed!

Herein lies the key to the life of the believer. This One who brought *"the eternal life which dwelt with the Father"* has now come to live within our lives! Ours is not the task of somehow being like Jesus; we are to embody His word, and in so doing, contain the "splendour" of the Son of God! The revelation of God is *always* through the Son; the only means which we have to reveal God is by possessing and being possessed by the Son. Christ in us, and we in Christ: becoming "shaped to the likeness of his son," we also become revealers of the Within One (Rom. 8:29). As a lovely trophy on the mantle exists only to point to the excellence of its owner, so we exist that "he might display in the ages to come how immense are the resources of his grace, and how great is his kindness to us in Christ Jesus" (Eph. 2:7). There is something unique about Himself that He wishes to express through each separate person!

There are different kinds of people. There are brilliant people and others whose minds are dull. There are both those who are emotionally stable and unstable, strong willed and weak willed, some whose bodies are beautiful and some with bodies unseemly and unsightly. But every single human being has the capacity to uniquely demonstrate certain qualities of the Spirit of God in this world.

A little child with a retarded mind comes to attend the worship service. She sometimes sits on the front row, with her blinded mind unable to comprehend the message. After the service, she puts her arms around the pastor's neck and kisses his cheek. She is revealing something of God through her life which cannot be revealed by a brilliant attorney in the same congregation. The attorney, in turn, presents another clue to the nature of God which can be revealed only through a man with a brilliant mind.

God made every human being on the face of this earth for one reason: *in order that He might dwell within him, revealing Himself through him.*

The important conclusion is that men were created by God in order that they too might be a part of His total revelation about

Himself. When the Spirit of Christ becomes the Inner Self within our lives, He begins to show the world something of Himself through us.

Second Corinthians 4:6 teaches, "For the same God who said, 'Out of darkness let light shine,' has caused his light to shine within us, to give the light of revelation—the revelation of the glory of God in the face of Jesus Christ." Scripture also teaches, "In Him we live and move and have our being" . . . "He fills all things" . . . "God is all and in all." Romans 8:16 adds this powerful statement: "In that cry the Spirit of God joins with our spirit . . ." Think of it! The within one that is Ralph Neighbour and the Within One that is God are to be fully united in testifying that we are God's children, and if children, then heirs. There is a marvelous union here. God made mankind with bodies, intellects, wills, and emotions. He made each man in order that he might spontaneously be inhabited by "the within one" called "the spirit of a man," *and* the "Inner Self" who is the Spirit of Christ.

This is why we are on this earth! This is why we are put in our separate places. We were made by God to be inhabited by Him, for He uses humans to reveal His greatest qualities: love, mercy, justice, gentleness. You cannot see love by looking at the Grand Canyon, and you don't see patience in an atom or the stars. You don't see meekness in the flower growing in the forest. You see those qualities of God only when you look at a person who is inhabited by God.

Notice Romans 8:19: "For the created universe waits with eager expectation for God's sons to be revealed." The Greek word for "created universe" used in this verse refers to rocks, trees, rivers, and mountains—all inanimate objects. Imagine! The rest of this universe, already revealing the Inner Presence of God, cries out, "Man, highest order of our Lord's creation, when will you finally join us in revealing the Within One?" Even the inanimate world realizes there is something of God the world cannot know until we become the sons of God, until His presence is within our spirits so that our minds, emotions, wills, and bodies no longer express our own self-life, but the Within One.

If we prostitute what God has planned for us by creating "power blocks" of personal influence, we commit the greatest sin of all. You and I have no right to choose an area in which "my influence" will be spread, in which "my power" will control, in which "my intellect" becomes the important factor. If we radiate a sphere of personal power and influence, we have missed the whole point of our reason-for-being on this earth.

We are not here to build reputations, to have "benevolent influence" upon the world, or to "do some good thing" that people will remember, or even benevolently finance institutions so that our names might be inscribed on their buildings. We are put on this earth for one purpose only, and that is for God to reveal Himself through us. Christians are those who voluntarily invited the God of the universe, the Holy Spirit, revealed by the Son of God named Jesus, to live inside their lives. George will reveal something of the nature of God in Christ that Robert cannot, but Robert reveals something of God in the quality of life he lives in Christ that his dear wife, Joyce, cannot reveal. So it goes, to the smallest child in the world.

What Is a Christian?

An authentic Christian is one who has a resident boss—"the Spirit of God . . . the Spirit of Christ . . . the Spirit of the Father . . . the Spirit of Him who raised Jesus from the dead . . . the God who raised Jesus from the dead . . . the Holy Spirit . . ." living in him, in order that God might "mind His own business" in his life. Consider 2 Corinthians 3:18. Previous verses tell about Moses coming down from the mountain after having met God and how the Israelites put a veil over his face because of its radiance. Paul then says, ". . . for us there is no veil over the face, we all reflect as in a mirror the splendour of the Lord; thus we are transfigured into his likeness, from splendour to splendour; such is the influence of the Lord who is Spirit."

What is a Christian? It is a person who has ceased living for self, who has become the temple of God. A human is born in order that the Inner Self, the Holy Spirit, might so consume and possess him from the spirit to the soul and body that he will remain upon the earth simply to reveal "the Within One" of the universe.

Paul's "great secret" in Colossians 2 was a secret hidden for long generations, now revealed to us. That secret was this: *Christ lives within us, as the hope of glory.* In 1 John 4:12 John says, "Though God has never been seen by any man, God himself dwells in us . . ." Perhaps the most beautiful of these Christ-in-you passages is 2 Corinthians 1:20 ff:

> "He is the Yes pronounced upon God's promises, every one of them. That is why, when we give glory to God, it is through Christ Jesus that we say 'Amen.' And if you and we belong to Christ, guaranteed as his and anointed, it is all God's doing; it is God also who have set his seal upon us, and as a pledge of what is to come *has given the Spirit to dwell in our hearts.*"

God made our body to be a Holy Temple, in order that He might be the God who fills His temple. The One who called Himself the Vine made us to be the branches. He said, "Just be connected to me, and I will flow my life through you. There will be fruit on the branch that comes directly from Me, without your doing another thing."

"I am His body," shared Paul in 1 Corinthians 12:12. As Paul lived in his body, even also did the Son of God. Paul knew that the Godhead in all of His greatness lived in him, in order that He might express himself.

What have you done with *your* life? Do you acknowledge that you are a person made for God to express the highest of all His qualities? What have you done with your life? In order for the love of God to emanate from your life, He had to give you the freedom to voluntarily say, "Spirit of the Universe, living in the highest levels of the stars I can see with my naked eye and living in the tiniest little bug I can see on the ground, Oh, Spirit of God Who fills all things, *fill me too!* You have something to reveal to this world that can only be revealed as I yield myself to You. Spirit of Christ, take my life, my body, my mind, my emotions, my will; take the very spirit of me that lives within me for Yourself. I am yours to express whatever You wish to express."

In 2 Corinthians 4:6-7, men are likened to pots of earthenware used in ancient times to contain a rare deed or document. Such pots were made only in order that they might at last be broken when the full document was needed. In our lives it is not until we "pots of earthernware" are broken that the Spirit of Christ can be fully revealed. God made us to be "pots of earthernware" to contain Him as a treasure.

There must be a point in time when I choose the will of God in the place of my will, regardless of the consequences or what the reaction of others might be. Furthermore, God does not promise that if I will be broken, the reward will be continually joyous experiences. Job learned that for him to be in the middle of God's will meant to have everything removed—family, friends, health, and wealth. Everything was taken away, but it made no difference, for God was revealing something of Himself to the world through Job's agony and pain. These qualities could not be revealed to the world by a rich Job, sitting in the luxury of his wealth and his cattle with his lovely family gathered around him. God wanted to reveal a quality to the world through Job which could be done only through his personal agony and suffering; that revelation now stands as a comfort to all mankind! Thank you, Job, for letting the Lord use you. You revealed Him to us all.

To be filled with His Spirit, to choose the will of God, to be a container for Him, means we must be ready to be anything He chooses to make of us.

The story is told of an older minister who was trying to teach a young minister an important lesson. He said to the young man, "I want you to go to the casket in the mortuary. I want you to speak to that dead man stretched out in the casket. Tell him every loving thing you imagine those who love him might say to him."

The man did so. He spoke words of love, sweetness, and commendation, and then returned to the manse.

The older minister asked, "Was there any response from the dead man in the coffin?"

He said, "No, none at all."

Replied his teacher, "I want you to go back to the dead man.

This time speak to him as though you were the embodiment of all the enemies he has in this world. I want you to hurl at him every evil, malevolent, bitter, insulting thing which comes to your mind."

The younger minister did so, returning to report he had accomplished the assignment.

The older minister said to him, "Was there any response from the man in the coffin?"

He replied, "No, there was no response at all."

Said the tutor, "So shall you react to praise and criticism, my son, when you are buried with Christ to let His life alone live through you."

Here is an important lesson which must be learned by all who wish to be a broken vessel: one must become totally and completely surrendered before God will reveal His Life, His Person, His Inner Self. He needs nothing at all from us. Our death is all He needs in order to express Himself. The carnal Christian who determines that his body, mind, emotions, and will shall reveal both God and self is doomed to frustration. God has called every Christian to be totally and completely dead to self, broken from his own desires and plans. He wishes to reveal "all the fulness of the Godhead bodily" in us and through us. This is a deep thought, but connected to it is the most important part of the concept of Spirit-filled evangelism.

WHAT IS "WITNESS"?

If we say that witness is "bearing testimony," we are missing the whole point of Scripture. Witness is not anything I do for God. The word "witness" in Greek is *marturia.* It refers to one who is *totally yielded,* involved in being so used by God that he is ready to die as a martyr. The definition of marturia is "one who furnishes evidence."

Is a witness someone who goes around with salvation tracts, saying to sinners, "Look. I want you to read this page and then this page." No, that is not necessarily the work of a witness. Distributing gospel tracts is a good thing, and I do it, but let us understand that this is not witnessing.

In the purest biblical sense, a witness is one who has within him the presence of the Almighty God, who constantly furnishes evidence that within there is more than self. "Within me, Christ dwells! God, the Holy Spirit, is in me!"

Witness takes place when any Christian, in any situation in his life, spontaneously communicates that he contains more than self. When this witness uses words, we call it "testimony," but witness is more than testimony. Witness can also include sharing the written Word or "explaining the plan of salvation," but more than even that is involved.

So many Christians today think they can be a self-centered individual, and yet by simply giving a testimony or using a good high-pressure evangelism technique they will perform the work of God. Some preachers feel that if they preach a sermon with a great deathbed illustration at the end which gets people coming down the aisle they are "proclaiming." Not so! This can well be simply an act of *flesh doing something for God.*

Good old consecrated self loves to boast, "I had so many saved this week, or I had so many saved in the revival meeting." For a clergyman to speak like this is a heartbreaking thing, for clergymen do not bring people to Christ. Among us today is the heresy that there are some preachers who are more holy than others, who as a result see more people "walk the aisle" in their services.

Our generation needs to be protected from the professional clergyman who performs certain "ministries" for God that the *laos,* the simple men or women of God, are not qualified to do. That is not true! We are all the ministers of God, for all who are genuinely His children and have known the release of the Spirit of God within their lives are ministers—and all ministers are witnesses. He who is within me declares Himself, day by day and hour by hour.

From Acts 1:8 it is clear we cannot be witnesses until the indwelling Holy Spirit manifests Himself: "Tarry in Jerusalem until *after* the Holy Spirit is come upon you, and then you will be my witnesses." In John 15:26-27, Jesus promised He would send His

Holy Spirit into the world to "witness to me. And you also are my witnesses, because you have been with me from the first."

What witness does God give me? It is simply a declaration that I am more than myself. I confess that the Within One has come to possess my life, to own it, to operate it, to control it. I can now pass out a tract, preach a sermon, serve on a mission field, become an education director, a music director, a Sunday School teacher (the list of things to be done is endless), and the Inner Person of the universe will always be revealing Himself as a river of water flowing from my life.

WHAT IS THE ROLE OF THE HOLY SPIRIT IN WITNESSING?

Paul had this in mind when he wrote 2 Corinthians 13:3-5:

> "Then you will have the proof you seek of the Christ who speaks through me, the Christ who, far from being weak with you, makes his power felt among you. True, he died on the cross in weakness, but he lives by the power of God; and we who share his weakness shall by the power of God live with him in your service.
>
> Examine yourselves: are you living the life of faith? Put yourself to the test. Surely you recognize that Jesus Christ is among you?— unless of course you prove unequal to the test."

What is a witness? *A witness is one who can no longer be himself!* He finds himself inhabited by the Holy Spirit of God, the indwelling Spirit of Christ. All he does at work, at home, at play bears the evidence of that fact. That is "witness." Witness is more than living according to a certain pattern; it is simply the very person of God within me, revealing something of Himself in all that I am and in all that I do, in every situation.

When I am not witnessing, I am in a situation in which the Spirit of God is not free to reveal Himself because I won't let Him.

In John 16:8-11 we discover that the Spirit of God is in the world acting independently of me, convicting unbelievers: ". . . and [he shows] where wrong and right and judgment lie. He will convict them of wrong . . . he will convince them that right

is on my side . . . and he will convince them of divine judgment."
The Holy Spirit moves directly within the life of unbelievers, revealing God's presence in the world.

Note the three truths the Holy Spirit performs without your help: *He convicts of sin and judgment and righteousness.* When, however, He is ready to reveal the highest quality of God—love—He does it through human beings who have become containers for the Indwelling One.

God is love, and God is Spirit. His Spirit of Christ is love living within me. I cannot fake this. I cannot conjure up this emotion. When you work closely with some churchmen, you discover there is no love for people in their heart. The finest Bible teachers, well prepared and eloquent, often lack this witness of Christ within, for there is no love in their lives. The essence of God within the life will be overflowing love.

I have a mole on my cheek, and so does my father. I have the voice of my father in my throat. I never wonder if I am an adopted son. I know I am the son of my father because I have his physical characteristics. They are in my voice, on my cheek, in the habits of my body, and in all of the attitudes of my life.

So it is with the Christian. We have the Son of God dwelling within our lives. He will reveal Himself in the very characteristics of our natures. It does not matter whether we are drinking coffee with a friend or refusing to make a business deal where a little gouging might make the profit soar; the Spirit of Christ within me will reveal Himself as the resident boss of my life.

Not long ago a young mother named Linda had the joy of helping Hazel come to know Jesus. Hazel went back to the home where she lived with her husband and children. Hazel was different. Her husband could not understand what the difference was. They were attending our TOUCH ministry for parents of retarded children. As he observed his wife with some of the Christians there, David could not understand what had happened to Hazel. Finally he went to her and said, "You know, I think a screw has come loose inside you somewhere. I think maybe *you* are becoming mentally retarded. You don't scream at me anymore. I don't understand you!" The Within One was revealing Himself through Hazel. She was just a little "baby Christian," without ability to verbalize her conversion experience to her husband, but the "witness" was profound. A few nights later, Linda's husband, Bob, walked over and visited with David. Because of the witness of the Holy Spirit within Hazel, David had discovered the reality of the living Christ. With Bob serving as the spiritual obstetrician, David was born again. When we visited him two nights later, David said to me, "You know, this new life is really amazing. I don't even cuss under my breath at my boss anymore."

A new life is within that spirit of David. That life will continue to grow and expand within until David's whole life will be transformed. He will look back in later years and say, "I can't believe I ever used to live a sinful, selfish life; I cannot imagine why I ever was another kind of person."

The Within One is the key to all witness. The Holy Spirit is not the one who *helps us* witness; the Holy Spirit *is* the witness. All He needs from you to witness through you is *nothing*. If you will be nothing, He can be everything. Whenever you try to "be something," to that degree you diminish His witness. You may stand before throngs and demonstrate how eloquent you are in speech, but you diminish His witness in the display of your ability. Demonstrate how generous you may be, but be certain you do not witness in a generosity born of the self-life instead of the Christ-life. All He needs from us is nothing.

Several years ago, I shared in a week of preaching at a Baptist church in Tyler, Texas. On Tuesday night I met Lou Ann, a high school senior with an I.Q. that must have been on the genius level. She said to me, "I have been reading a certain author's writings." When she mentioned the name of the author, my heart sank. The writer in question had received her material from the middle kettle of hell! She has written the most devilish, anti-God, atheistic literature I have ever read. Lou Ann said, "I have read all her books. I have been her disciple for the last three years. In my *mind,* I have decided she is right: there is no God. There cannot be! But I came to this service and sat here tonight with these people, and something in my *heart* tells me God is truly here. I have felt such love in this place. Would you help me? I have decided tonight that there must be a God, but I can't find him."

We made an appointment for Saturday morning at 9:00. She came to the pastor's office, and we began to visit. I tried to help her intellectually, for this is where she chose to begin her search for the reality of God. I shared the teleological, cosmological, and ontological reasons for believing in God. I moved on to what had touched the logical mind of C. S. Lewis in *Mere Christianity,* the greatest explanation of the Christian faith I have ever read.

At 11:00 that morning—two hours later—Lou Ann finally looked at me and said, "I'm sorry, Ralph. You have tried so hard. But I tell you in all honesty that I am not one inch closer to knowing Him now than when we started talking. I just can't find Him."

In frustration and in pain I replied, "Lou Ann, I am sorry I have failed you, and I confess to you that your intelligence is far beyond mine. But, little lady, please keep searching, for I know that God is real. Do not take my failure to lead you to Him as the ultimate conclusion that you cannot find Him. Lou Ann, let me tell you how real God is to me. I have three boys in Dallas, and I love them very deeply. This is the first day of fishing season. I know Ralph Neighbour better than you know Ralph Neighbour, and I know that the man who lives inside this carcass is a pretty selfish kind of man. I know he cares infinitely more about his three sons than he cares about a strange teen-age girl in Tyler he will never see again. I see myself sitting here on a Saturday morning instead of fishing with the boys I love; I observe myself working as hard as I have ever worked, mentally and physically, spending two solid hours trying to help you find an Almighty God who loves you. Lou Ann, Ralph Neighbour does not do that! There is no way I can explain, even to myself, why I should spend *five minutes* with you. Apart from the presence of Christ in my life, I would not be doing what I am doing right now. If it were not for the God who lives in me, I wouldn't give you a split second of my time. That's the way my own selfish nature operates. But I tell you honestly, if I thought it would help, I would stay here until midnight to talk with you. Only a very real Person living within me could possibly be responsible for this!"

At that point her eyes exploded with tears. She said, "It is true! There is a God!" In a moment she regained her composure; her next words did not seem at first to be suitable in a minister's office, but even as she said them, I realized that no other vocabulary could really say for her what needed to be said. These were her words: "Ralph, if it were not for the fact that God is in you, you would not give a damn about me, would you?"

"Damn" had hardly been a theological word for me until that moment, but suddenly only that word seemed *right* to me! Nothing else was strong enough. No other word could communicate what we both knew she meant, and I realized that what she was saying was absolutely true.

I took her hand between my two hands and said, "Lou Ann, it is so true! If He did not live within me, this self-centered person they call Ralph Neighbour would, in all truthfulness, not give a *damn* about you."

She said, "Ralph, I know now He is real!" She quietly dropped to her knees and invited Christ to become resident boss in her life.

What reached Lou Ann? All my logic, all my years spent in seminary working through all the problems relating to the existence of God, meant nothing to her. She was TOUCHed by the simple revelation that I had become a temple for the Living God who loved when I could not.

That's what "witness" is. And you can't fake it!

NOTES

1. I am deeply indebted to the writing of Norman Grubb for the concepts shared in this chapter.

Chapter 3
The World of "TOUCH"

The God who created the world and everything in it, and who is Lord of heaven and earth, does not live in shrines made by men. It is not because he lacks anything that he accepts service at men's hands, for he is himself the universal giver of life and breath and all else. He created every race of men of one stock, to inhabit the whole earth's surface. He fixed the epochs of their history and the limits of their territory. They were to seek God, and, it might be, *touch and find him;* though indeed he is not far from each one of us, for in him we live and move, in him we exist (Acts 17:24-28 author's italics).

For years American society has been divided in its attitude toward the church. On one hand, there have been *members* of churches and those who were at least sympathetic to the life and message of the church and, on the other hand, there have been the *"Outsiders":* those who have either rejected the church or who have not had enough exposure to it to be concerned about what it teaches and preaches.

As a "Preacher's Kid" growing up in the parsonage, I was quite familiar with the "Revivals," "Sunday School Enlargement Campaigns," and "Weekly Visitation Programs" in the church. These activities nearly always resulted in some people receiving Christ.

Later on, as a youthful minister, I threw myself wholeheartedly into the use of these programs. I believed that Christ could reach the world, but only through such ministries.

It took a while, but I gradually began to recognize that *the only people the church was reaching were those who were already "church oriented."* In fact, from the boyhood shelter of Dad's parsonage, I considered 95 percent of the total population to be "church oriented." Undoubtedly there are some Bible-belt agricultural communities where this might be true, but the first week I worked in a factory as a college student I became aware that this was not true in the city!

What churches do makes precious little impact upon Outsiders! With each passing year, the problem of evangelizing non-churched Americans increases, for *they have now grown to represent more than 60% of the American population.* The endless hours invested by Christians in their traditional programs have little or no influence upon them. As a middle-aged minister, I am now greatly distressed by the fact that many Christians do not seem to be concerned by the total lack of rapport we have with Outsiders!

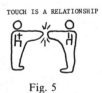

TOUCH IS A RELATIONSHIP

Fig. 5

We are not TOUCHing a huge segment of the community with the gospel of Christ. We have no "TOUCH point"—no contact point with them. Dr. David P. Haney, author of *Renew My Church,* calls this the "Cinderella Syndrome." [1] That is, the church is carrying about a single-size shoe, and only as it fits can the church help a person in his walk with God. The great mass, however, cannot wear it! A limited front produced limited contact and, consequently, limited results.

How many "Outsiders" live in your community? To discover the answer, you might compare the seating capacities of all church sanctuaries in your town to the total population. After subtracting the number of empty pews on a given Sunday morning, you will arrive at a staggering figure. It will become apparent that Outsiders represent a huge proportion of the population.

Better yet, "play hooky" some Sunday morning from the worship service and go door-knocking. See how many homes there are with someone to answer the door. Observe the children riding their bicycles. Estimate how many of the not-at-home houses you approach have emptied their occupants to boating, pleasure, trips, etc. We live in a world of Outsiders!

What is your church doing to reach them? Your Sunday School will attract only a few of them. Fine preaching in a lovely sanctuary means nothing to them. And further, *our churches have few, if any, plans for TOUCHing the lives of Outsiders* if they will not fit into our program of coming to church. There is simply no point of contact established!

THE FIRST THING AN UNBELIEVER DOES IS TOUCH CHRIST. THEN, WHEN HE KNOWS HIM, HE NEXT MUST TRUST HIM AS LORD AND SAVIOR.

Why do Outsiders avoid our lovely church buildings and stimulating programs? There are a thousand answers—Some emotional, some spiritual, others intellectual, social, or physical. One Outsider may have been insulted by a Sunday School teacher as a child and consequently "gave up God for Lent." Another may have been influenced by an atheist father. There is a woman too shy to mix with crowds; there is another woman ashamed of her divorced condition. Here lives a hedonist, there a pragmatist, and over there a humanist. All of them . . . Outsiders!

Let us face this fact clearly: all of them are avoiding our lovely buildings and well-organized programs. If we don't face it, they will live their lives through without ever being TOUCHed by the Christian message!

God has given His church many excellent ways by which the gospel of Christ can be communicated to America's non-church

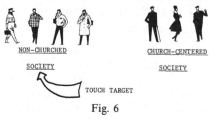

Fig. 6

oriented society. This book presents one of them. It emphasizes establishing POINTS OF CONTACT with Outsiders. We call these points of contact *TOUCH POINTS.*

PRINCIPLE #1: TOUCH ALWAYS HAPPENS OUTSIDE CHURCH BUILDINGS

The church is not TOUCHing the Outsider from within its buildings, but we devote practically all of our Christian service to the things which happen inside their walls. The typical Baptist church averages over 300 hours a year equipping members for activity *inside* the building. (This includes all the choir rehearsals, Deacon's meetings, Church Training, Sunday School meetings, and committee meetings ad nauseum.) *The average church does not provide as much as twelve hours a year to equip Christians to witness for Christ outside church walls!*

Yet, it is there that Christians spend most of their lives—outside those walls, at home, school, work, or play. Furthermore, churches that *do* offer personal evangelism training rarely have an effective strategy for reaching the Outsider. (Remember the definition of an "Outsider"!) The visitation program works well in reaching church-oriented families, *but it does not offer a TOUCH point to reach Outsiders.*

PRINCIPLE #2: TOUCH POINTS ARE NEEDED

Mark well this next statement: TOUCH POINTS must be developed around the NEED of the Outsider before there will be an effective transmission of the MESSAGE of Christ's love. Example: A Christian casually says to an Outsider he barely knows, "Would you like to have a full and meaningful life?" The Outsider says to himself as he turns and walks away, "I'd much rather know how to face the fact that my doctor has given me three weeks to live!" The Outsider had a *need;* that Christian could have been a thousand times more effective if he had taken time to *discover that need,* and express the gospel as the answer to the real problem.

All Outsiders have needs. Shattered hearts, broken homes, unhappiness in jobs, troubled children—the list of needs is endless;

but one-shot church visits won't discover those needs! Know the Outsider lovingly enough to understand his hang-up or his heart-ache, and through that portal you can drive a semi-truckload of the gospel, straight into his life.

THE WORD "TOUCH" HAS DISTINCTIVE MEANING
"TOUCH" stands for . . .

T   ransforming
O   thers
U   nder
C   hrist's
H   and

"TOUCH" is your life, controlled by the Christ who loves, carry-ing His-life-in-you to confront an Outsider.

THE TOUCH EMBLEM HAS THE SAME MEANING

Erwin Hearne, a Christian artist famous for his paintings of Baptist history, prayerfully designed this emblem to express the concept of TOUCH. It uses a white dove to represent the Holy Spirit, resting above a red heart, representing the Christian's spirit: the Holy Spirit in my spirit. The wearer of such an emblem must be Spirit-filled; otherwise, it has no meaning!

Fig. 7

This emblem has been worn by Christians, embossed on jackets, shirts, pins, tie tacks, even key chains. Along with the word "TOUCH," it is used to identify "People Who Care" to Outsiders. In some situations it is extremely effective to use the word "Touch" and the accompanying symbol in relating to Outsiders, rather than to use the name of a church.

For example, in the Houston area there exists a TOUCH ministry to "Night People." Men wear blue nylon jackets bearing the TOUCH symbol. Among other establishments, they regularly visit the beer joints in the area. If one of these men should begin to share in conversation with an Outsider in one of these bars, the use of the words "Baptist church" would probably terminate the friendship. The reasons are legion. Perhaps the person is a staunch member of another religious group. More likely, the Outsider in the bar does not identify the word "Baptist" with Christ's *forgiveness, grace,* and *mercy.* In Houston, Texas, experience has proved that the word "Baptist" is linked in the minds of many Outsiders only to bitter political fights which have been waged against the legalization of liquor in the state. Other regions have similar connotations. Without question, Christian men are opposed to the liquor traffic . . . but there is a difference between hating sin and *loving sinners!* One does not have to approve of a man's habits to find the ability to love him by faith!

When these Christian men are developing a love-relationship through the indwelling Christ with an Outsider at a bar, the crucial issue is not the man's *liquor,* but his *redemption.* Let that Outsider meet Christ in a personal way, and he will help fight liquor—but in his present unregenerate state he cannot accept any part of that concept! First the Christian must be able to share with him the good news that Jesus lives, that His children are "The People Who Care," that this Son of God wants to live in everyone's life. The use of the symbol and of the word TOUCH identifies the bearer simply as a Spirit-filled Christian. For the Outsider, at the beginning of the relationship, that is enough.

Once a person meets Christ, he will wish to be a part of The Family of God and will join a church. Many personal, practical experiences have proven that countless Outsiders could be reached if we church-oriented people would stop alienating them with the emotionally-loaded labels and structures which serve only to drive them away before they hear about Christ.

The emblem and the word represent the simple truth of any vital Christian witness: *The Holy Spirit has come to live in my spirit!*

TOUCH DOES NOT START WITH A PROGRAM

How many ways will the Holy Spirit utilize to TOUCH non-church-related people? *Hundreds and hundreds of ways.* That is why

TOUCH does not start with a "program." It starts with Christ in the believer.

A Christian must prayerfully discover how the Spirit will lead him to TOUCH unbelievers. It is a very personal matter. When Christians take TOUCH Training, they are made to understand that they will be expected to prayerfully discover what the Holy Spirit would have them to do in sharing their faith with Outsiders. They are told that . . .

PRINCIPLE #3: WE ALREADY HAVE TOUCH BUILT INTO OUR LIVES

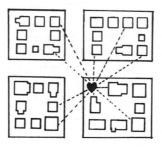

Fig. 8

For example, you may be the only Holy-Spirit-in-the-heart kind of person in your entire neighborhood. Who are the people who live around you? Across the street is a family with children who do not go to church, or perhaps they attend a non-evangelical church on Sunday. They will not ever ride a church bus to your local Sunday School, attend a revival, or even give answers in a survey. They are from an Outsider family. Why not start a Tuesday afternoon Bible Club for them in the den of your own home, using materials that are readily available to tell them about Jesus? Experience has proved that those youngsters will usually attend a one-hour "TOUCH Time" in a neighborhood home, even when parents do not permit them to go to church. Many TOUCH Time clubs already exist, and some are reaching as many as twenty or thirty children on a weekday afternoon.

Look around your neighborhood again: do you see teenagers? Why not start a "Rap Session" for them? Another possibility is a Neighborhood Bible Study for mothers. This is one of the most effective new ministries to Outsiders which Christians have available today. These are only a few of the many ways a neighborhood can be infiltrated and made God-conscious.

It is appalling to occasionally hear a church staff member say, "I am against a Bible study that 'Meets over there in a house!' It will become *competition to the church* [whatever that means!] and the next thing you know, we are going to have a church starting 'over there' in competition with what goes on in Our Building." That is utterly preposterous! If that church staff member would only consider the Neighborhood Bible Study in the same light he considers a Sunday School class meeting in his Sunday School building, it would not be one bit threatening and would be a powerful TOUCH point within the community of Outsiders now being ignored!

At West Memorial Baptist Church in Houston, we have tried to limit the proportion of believers to Outsiders in our Neighborhood Bible Studies. We try to allow only two Christian women from our church to participate in any one group. The balance of those who enter the Bible study should be unbelieving women—*Outsiders*—within the community. After all, the purpose is to develop a TOUCH point—not to develop new clusters of Happy Christians who are insulated from the unbeliever!

A TOUCH ministry could be developed by inviting everybody in the neighborhood to a "Block Party" or to a picnic held in someone's back yard. By using the Quaker Questions (see chap. 5), initial relationships with Outsiders can then be developed for further contacts.

Men of the neighborhood can be reached through golfing, fishing, and other recreational activities. There are literally scores of intimate life-to-life related ways God could use to reach neighborhoods for Jesus Christ, to reach those who are not interested in attending worship services. All He needs are some warm bodies who are ready to choose His will in the place of self-will!

SOME OF US HAVE TOUCH BUILT INTO OUR LIFE-STYLE

Jeanne was a baton twirler.
Paul was a lawyer.
Rodney understands alcoholics.
Joe Lee was an addict.
Paula was divorced.
John and Sue had an exceptional child.
Bill was a hot rod enthusiast.
Jim loved to hunt and fish,
. . .and all had a TOUCH ministry as a result!
(Others joined them to form *TOUCH* Groups.)

A TOUCH ministry can focus not only upon where I live, but it may also focus upon my *life-style*.

For example, a very beautiful young mother said, "I was the State Champion Baton Twirler when I was in college. Do you suppose the Lord could use that?" Could He? Just imagine what that young woman could do by getting junior high school girls together for baton twirling lessons in her back yard. By advertising on the bulletin boards in neighborhood teen-age hangouts, she could contact girls who would be interested. She could teach those girls how to twirl batons, and then they could come into her house, flop down on the shag rug in her den, open bottles of Coke, receive copies of *Good News for Modern Man,* and have fifteen minutes of Bible study before they go home. A group of girls could be reached for Christ through the skill of baton twirling! God had given this talent to this little woman so that her life could TOUCH girls who might otherwise never be TOUCHed by His love!

Paul is an attorney. He wanted to join the TOUCH Night People ministry. For some time he was encouraged *not* to get into any special group TOUCH ministry because *his law practice was being richly used by God as a TOUCH with Outsiders!*

Rodney is [2] an alcoholic and led a group of Christians who TOUCHed alcoholics. He led his church to assist Alcoholics Anonymous to reach those who have this problem. It is an easy matter to help an alcoholic see through a discussion of A. A.'s Step Three in *The Twelve Steps* that this God, this "higher power" an alcoholic must believe in, is revealed fully only through Jesus Christ! [3]

Joe Lee was a heroin addict for years before he came to know Jesus Christ. He knew personally the life-style of a junkie. This former Outsider started a TOUCH half-way house called "The Giant Step." Other Christians became a TOUCH group, working alongside him, helping and winning hard-core heroin addicts to Christ.

Paula was divorced, and Paula knew some of the agony that a divorced woman goes through. She knew how trying it can be to face the loneliness, the emptiness of a dissolved marriage. She tried attending a church, but every program seemed to be focused around family units. Being a bit more attractive than the average woman her age, she also discovered to her dismay that she was something of a threat to some women in the church who were unhappy about her being around their husbands. Paula almost dropped out of church. Then she began to see that her life style could be used for the glory of God. The church had no ministry whatsoever to scores of divorcees in the area. As a result, she began a TOUCH group for divorcees, scheduling it to meet on Monday night. This gave her a TOUCH with other women going through various stages of loneliness, withdrawal, and misery. TOUCH Divorcee Groups are now functioning successfully. Divorced women themselves are responsible for them; they often meet in the apartments or houses of divorced women and TOUCH Outsiders in their time of deepest pain.

John and Sue had an "exceptional" child. It changed their life style! As Sue sat in the waiting room of the Clinic where her little girl received therapy three times a week, she found other lonely mothers who did not know how to cope with the problems surrounding the home which contains a child with severe learning disabilities. Through her insight, a TOUCH group was structured to win these Outsider parents to Christ. They meet on Thursday evenings, and nineteen parents attend the dialogue sessions.

Bill was a hot rod enthusiast. Could God use even that? Bill had a potential contact through his hobby with every teen-age boy interested in hot rods in his community! His two-car garage could become a TOUCH center for sharing Christ with many teen-age boys who wished to learn more about "souping up" their cars.

Jim loved to hunt and fish. Why could he not use his lodge and his boat as TOUCH Points with Outsiders, fellowshiping with them, helping them discover Christ's love?

All of these people had a TOUCH ministry as a result of their life style. In some but not all situations, other Christians could join them to form TOUCH Group ministries.

Sometimes TOUCH ministries will be *temporary,* rather than continuous. That is, they will perform a specific ministry for a specific period of time.

For example, in San Antonio, Texas, a carnival spirit takes over at the end of the Lenten season, when thousands of people pour into the streets for Fiesta. Here is an opportunity for a TOUCH ministry! Could you begin a TOUCH ministry in your area in connection with a rodeo or county fair? It does not cost much to set up a booth, where dialogue can take place.

A TOUCH lay witnessing crusade can be revolutionary. Laymen from a church on fire for God go to share in small-group witnessing sessions, sponsored by another church where the members are not yet really involved with Outsiders. In this way, the spirit of TOUCH can spread.

A July 4 "TOUCH Blitz" at a beach crowded with teen-agers could be another temporary TOUCH ministry. There are endless ways the Holy Spirit will use to communicate Christ outside church buildings!

For example, in a shopping center or a Mall a booth may be set up on Saturdays for the sale of gospel literature. A couple of small tables and $20.00 worth of Christian books is all that would be necessary . . . but the opportunity for *encounter* with Outsiders, for *dialogue,* for *witness* without being offensive will be built into the very act of explaining the "merchandise." (Book stalls are used by Communists in this fashion throughout the world. They also offer an excellent opportunity for sharing Christ!) In many of our smaller towns it may well be one of the most profitable ways to share Christ with those who live in the surrounding rural areas.

PRINCIPLE #4: ALL TOUCH MINISTRIES SHOULD BEGIN BECAUSE THE HOLY SPIRIT PLACES A BURDEN WITHIN SOME CHRISTIAN'S HEART

They will not be originated by announcing in a worship service, "We are going to start Bible studies. Would you all help out?" Those who participate in TOUCH will be "The Company of the Committed" within the church membership. By offering the TOUCH Basic Training Course, the "starters" are narrowed down over a six-week period to those who are committed enough to become involved in sharing Christ. Those who complete the course are directed to pray for God's leadership toward a specific ministry. They are not encouraged to "start a program," but to recognize there are many ways that they can represent Christ to Outsiders. They are encouraged to *seek their directions for ministry from the Holy Spirit.* It works!

Again and again men came to the TOUCH office at Castle Hills First Baptist Church in San Antonio, and with deep emotion said, "God is calling me to a specific ministry." One man who did so is a pilot, flying executives around for a private corporation. One day he said, "I have a burden for a family. God has touched me to TOUCH a family that lives near me on our block." A prayer meeting set him apart to reach that family. That was his TOUCH ministry, to win that family! That is a great start for a man who had not done much witnessing for Christ before. Imagine what further ministry he will discover in later weeks as God enlarges his compassion to see the scene of his employment as a TOUCH point.

Malcolm saw South Vietnamese officers arriving in his town to learn how to speak English. He knew they needed to learn about Christ's love during the six months they would be in the United States; another TOUCH ministry was born! His church later bought a bus for him to use to transport them from place to place. Many returned to their Buddhist families as committed Christians. Malcolm now TOUCHes people he has never met through those converts.

Betty Lou found still another TOUCH for Christ through the leadership of the Holy Spirit. Betty Lou and her husband, Paul, own a farm one hour away from their home. She said to her clergyman, "The Lord is leading me to minister to unsaved children at our farm by providing a Day Camp for them." She got nearby farmers to loan her baby animals for a Children's Barnyard. She found other fellow soldiers among "The People Who Care" to work with her, and she had an Instant Witness to forty-eight Outsider children! The staff discovered that only eleven of the children had ever read John 3:16 before that time! Betty Lou's TOUCH group ministered to various age groups for three weeks, from 8:00 in the morning until 5:00 at night. Many made decisions!

Ernest is a fine surgeon. As he read *The Cross and the Switchblade*, he realized that Christ was burdening his heart about the problem of drug abuse. He began to pray for wisdom as he initiated the ministry. Led by the Holy Spirit, he began a ministry which would reach dozens of heroin addicts. Mexican physicians have heard of his project and asked him to arrange for his TOUCH program to be started in Mexico City; inquiries have also come from physicians in Europe about what God has done through him.

TOUCH MINISTRIES BEGIN WITH THE HOLY SPIRIT STARTING TO WORK IN SOMEBODY'S HEART!

Some Christians will be called to join in a ministry originally inspired in the heart of someone else. For instance, Malcolm needed help with his Internationals. Betty Lou needed many co-workers with her Day Camp. Ernest needed a whole team of Christians, both physicians and laymen, to help him in his work with addicts. One person received a calling to minister to a certain group; out of that burden others heard the Holy Spirit call, and another TOUCH group was born.

Special orientation must be provided for some TOUCH ministries; others require no training at all. It is not difficult to provide this advanced training. Most communities have skilled people who can provide directions.⁴ Usually one to six hours of training will be all that will be necessary to train a TOUCH group.

"Basic Training," however, should be required of all participants, primarily to screen those who will not stick with a ministry over a long period of time.

Even more important than this Basic Training Course, however, is participation in the Spirit-filled life, the yielded life, the life in which Jesus Christ is given absolute freedom to live and work within! Remember . . . .TOUCH is not an *organization;* it is a *relationship,* and it must begin *with a Spirit-filled life.* Unless a Christian is simply overflowing with the "rivers of water" Jesus referred to in John 7:38, he is not going to be able to communicate the indwelling Christ to an unbeliever. TOUCH is not a program! It is a relationship which exists between a believer filled with Christ's Spirit, and Outsiders. TOUCH is simply a Christ-filled life revealing The Within One to a self-filled life.

The first thing an unbeliever will do is TOUCH Christ. The problems created by flesh-centered evangelism today result because Christians do not understand this truth! It is impossible to win Outsiders to Christ when they have never had a chance to TOUCH Him.

Where can they go to TOUCH Him? It is true that they can read the Bible and TOUCH Him. Upon this conviction, the Sunday School has functioned since the beginning of the nineteenth century. Yet, the Bible itself explains that *Bible study is not the most "biblical" way for an unbeliever to TOUCH Christ!* The Bible we use to learn about the Incarnate Word, the Bible itself, teaches us that there is a greater way of witness within this world than that which is limited to Bible study. In John 5:39 Jesus said, "You study the scriptures diligently, supposing that in having them you have eternal life; *yet, although their testimony points to me, you refuse to come to me for that life."* (How many Sunday School teachers have "turned off" young people by teaching truths not experiential in their own lives?)

Christ *Himself* is a Living Presence in this world, and He is minding His own business within every human being who is filled with His Spirit. An Outsider TOUCHes Christ every time he TOUCHes a Spirit-filled life. Then, when he is aware that Christ lives in his world, he can trust Him as Lord and Savior. *First there has to be the TOUCH.* Next, there has to be an *understanding* of *who Christ is* in order that the ultimate objective, *trusting* Christ, can occur.

Any congregation which has Spirit-filled laity, located in a community containing Outsiders not being reached by traditional building-centered activities, should prayerfully consider beginning a TOUCH Ministry . . . *at once!*

NOTES

1. David P. Haney, *Renew My Church* (Grand Rapids: Zondervan Publishing House, 1972).

2. Not "was." Any honest alcoholic will always use the *present tense,* even though he has not touched a drop in years!

3. Step Three of the Twelve Steps says, ". . . made a decision to turn our will and our life over to the care of God as we understand Him."

4. An excellent book for use in sensitizing Christians to the need for TOUCH ministries is David P. Haney's *Renew My Church* (Grand Rapids: Zondervan Press, 1972). Note especially his chapter on "The Disciplined Walk."

Chapter 4
Understanding Outsiders

EPHESIANS 2—DEAD in sins and wickedness
    —Followed the evil ways of this present age
    —Obeyed the devil
    —Live sensually
    —Obeyed promptings of our own instincts and notions
    —Lay under the dreadful judgement of God
    —Separate from Christ
    —Strangers to the Covenant
    —A world without hope and without God
GALATIANS 3:22—Prisoners in subjection to sin.
    23—Close prisoners in the custody of the law
    4:8—The slaves of beings which in their nature are no gods
THERE IS NO HOPE IN THE OUTSIDER'S LIFE!

Consider the biblical description of an unbeliever, called in this book the "Outsider." [1] He is described in Ephesians as being "dead in sins," "outside God's control."

The best way to define the word *SIN* is to take away the *S* and the *N* and leave the unbent *I* living all by itself as the "resident boss" in the middle of a man's heart. All "sin" consists of is an

"I" condition! Because the Outsider has separated himself from God, he has "followed the evil ways of this present age." He has "obeyed the devil." He is "living sensually," meaning he lives without any interest in the things of the Spirit. He has "obeyed the promptings of his own instincts and emotions." He lives by his own desire. He now rests "under the dreadful judgment of God." He is "separate from Christ." He is a "stranger to the convenant." He lives in a "world without hope and without God!"

And, this is a miserable condition! If Christians fully comprehended the nature of this condition, there would be an urgency about the matter of sharing the indwelling Christ with Outsiders.

In the book of Galatians, additional statements are made which expand the Outsider's hopelessness. In chapters 3 and 4 of Galatians, Paul describes the Outsider as being a prisoner in subjection to sin. In Galatians 3:23 Paul enlarges on this by calling him a "close prisoner." This represents him as bound with manacles, ropes around his body, so that he has no ability whatsoever to move toward God. A close prisoner—and his jailer is the Law. Furthermore, in Galatians 4:8 Paul describes him as "a slave of beings which in their nature are no gods."

As Christians, we may decide to share Christ with this Outsider. How are we going to do that? How *can* we share Christ with a person in this condition? By using some little evangelistic program or some slick-paper presentation of the gospel? It will take much more than this because *there is no hope in the Outsider's life.* None! No hope whatsoever! What can man in his own strength possibly do to help him?

One of The People Who Care in Houston is a Spirit-filled psychiatrist, Dr. Juanita Hart.[2] One day I went to her and said, "Dr. Hart, I want you to describe the life of a lost man from the standpoint of his emotional problems." As a result, she developed the following diagram from one of her psychiatric journals. This is the cycle of an Outsider's life as a psychiatrist would look at it:

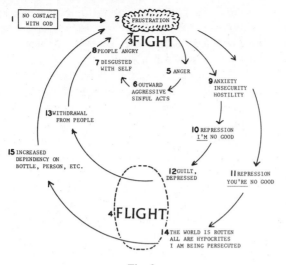

Fig. 9

SUMMARY

1. The Outsider's basic frustration: *no contact with God.*
2. The result: *frustration* of God's basic purpose for the life.
3-4. The two potential reactions to this frustration: *fight or flight.*
5. The root of frustration for the *fight* reaction.
6-8. The *fight* reaction analyzed.
9. The roots of frustration for the *flight* reaction.
10-11. The two limbs of *flight* reaction.
12-13. The "I'm No Good" limb analyzed.
14-15. The "You're No Good" limb analyzed.

We begin with the fact that this Outsider has *no contact with God* (1).[3] That is important to understand. The scriptures just reviewed emphasize this fact. Living with no contact with God whatsoever, there comes a horrible sense of emotional frustration within the life of an Outsider.

Norman Grubb was exactly right when he said there is one major reason for every one of us having been put on this earth: *to be a container for God.* [4] Here is our reason for being. We are created simply to contain God! When men live as empty containers, not filled with the presence of the One for Whom they were created, they are filled with frustration (2).

What does the Outsider do when he is frustrated? He faces crises to which he must react, but he cannot handle the stress of situations. Every Outsider reacts emotionally in one of two ways to the fact that he has no personal, rewarding contact with God: he may *fight* that frustration (3), or he may decide to *run away from it* (4). (Consider the Outsiders you already know who react precisely as described in the diagram.)

Many cope with estrangement from God by becoming *angry* (5). To illustrate the frustration, I recall watching a father playfully wrestling with his little boy on the couch one night. He put a "hammerlock" on his son so that he could not move. He was "a close prisoner of the law," and Daddy was the "law." After the boy wiggled and squirmed and could not get away, he finally found a burst of superhuman strength far beyond that of an eight year old. He said, "Let me *go!*"—and broke out of his father's hold. *Anger* gave him that strength.

Many times an Outsider, with anger controlling his life, will try to handle his frustration with powerful, aggressive sinful acts (6). He does things that shock others who watch. We must understand why: he is not at peace with God or himself. As a result of his action, he becomes disgusted with himself (7).

Perhaps someone may say to him, "You are a nice person. I'm going to be nice to you." When the Outsider doesn't like himself, it is almost impossible for him to accept the love offered by another. His response is to become outwardly aggressive, and he deliberately makes others angry at him so he will not be liked (8).

Do you know someone who acts like that? This is the action of one living in constant frustration, and *that frustration basically stems from the fact that the Outsider lives without meaningful contact with God. He was made to be a container for God,* and any lesser use of his life will always be unrewarding and frustrating.

The other way Outsiders will react is through the *pattern of flight*

(4). Instead of *fighting* his frustration, he may try to *run away from it*. In this case, the Outsider may choose between two cycles of emotion, both expressing forms of anxiety, hostility, and insecurity (9). He is afraid, feeling, "I don't know who I am. I don't know if people like me, and so I will be hostile to the world around me."

This anxiety and hostility and insecurity takes two possible courses; many times both will be adopted. The Outsider may decide either "I'm no good" (10) or "you're no good" (11). If a person says, "I'm no good," he feels guilty and becomes depressed (12). Running away from the frustration of being an empty Container, he thinks, "I don't have any contact with God; I guess I'm not worthy of any contact."

Many times Christians who minister to Outsiders in taverns through a TOUCH group observe people living in this pattern. The Outsider says, "Well, man, that religion stuff may be great for people who go to church, but I could not even picture someone like me going into a church building!" Feeling unworthy, he has withdrawn from church people (13).

Suicide may become a serious consideration to depressed Outsiders. Their thought pattern may be: "I'm anxious and insecure. I'm no good. I'm guilty. I don't deserve to live. I'll just destroy myself." This Outsider is in a *desperate* state. One who has such a "hole in the heart" may need not only spiritual help, but also medical assistance.

The other *flight* cycle, also resulting from insecurity, begins with the attitude that "you are no good" (11). Not long ago an Outsider said to a Christian friend, "I am just waiting for the time when you let me down! Everyone else in my life has done so. Sooner or later you will too!" Such a nontrusting attitude leads to heartbreak after heartbreak—and a total feeling of personal insecurity. This individual is not only saying, "I'm no good," but also saying, "No one else is any good either, and if I just wait long enough, the world will prove itself to be rotten. Everyone is a hypocrite" (14).

This individual may become increasingly dependent upon alcohol or drugs or may become possessively attached to one person, telephoning ten or twenty times a day with endless conversation (15). Sooner or later, the person recycles, going back again to the basic frustration of not being rightly controlled by God. Maybe the next time he will choose the *fight* cycle, or perhaps he may say, "I'm no good," and become suicidal. Perhaps the next time he will lash out against someone else. His entire spiritual problem focuses upon a *basic frustration: the Outsider has no contact with God, and he was created to contain God.*

When a Christian understands these cycles, he becomes aware of why he cannot, *in the flesh*, help an Outsider! What can human mind, emotion, and will do for this person? There is no hope for Outsiders, apart from Christ. Only Christ can help—and only when Christ is "resident boss" in your life can He use you to help!

When this generation of Christians accepts the fact that we cannot win people to Christ until *we* are first fully yielded to Him, we may see the greatest evangelistic thrust of our century! At present, we seem to think God can use a half-committed, carnal church member who has been given some training in how to witness to win the world. It won't work!

After directing Personal Evangelism Institutes in scores of cities, I have returned to those cities later, to find Christians still barren and impotent in the matter of witnessing. It broke my heart! I kept saying to myself, "Why? What is the matter?" Gradually I began to realize where the problem was: *I began to see that you cannot expect a person who is not Spirit-filled to reveal the presence of Christ to Outsiders!*

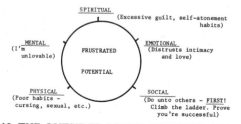

Fig. 10, THE OUTSIDER MEETS ANOTHER OUTSIDER

THE OUTSIDER'S SEARCH

When the totally frustrated Outsider, fighting and flighting, meets another Outsider, what does he find? Another frustrated life! He simply sees another "empty container" without God.

These Outsiders get together. They may meet in a club or a lodge, or even join the same church. They begin to try to help each other, even, though both of them are filled with excessive guilt, leading to self-atonement habits. Because they are both emotionally frustrated, they distrust intimacy and love. Socially, their attitude may be "Do unto others first! Climb the ladder! Prove you are successful!" Physically, they share poor habits, possibly including sexual immorality. Mentally, they are constantly thinking, "I am unlovable."

A recent teen-age "Rap Session" in Houston demonstrated the prevalence of this attitude among Outsiders. Within the group of eleven young unbelievers, eight of them were living with the same underlying emotional attitude: "I'm unlovable!" One who is Outside cannot help another who is Outside; yet the world is full of moralists who think it is possible.

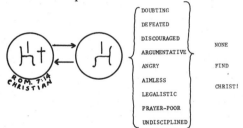

Fig. 11, THE OUTSIDER MEETS A CARNAL BELIEVER

Perhaps the Outsider meets a carnal Christian. Perhaps this man is a deacon in the church and a tither of his money; nevertheless, he proudly allows a great big Ego to sit on the throne of his life. He is a Romans-7:19 Christian! "The good which I want to do, I fail to do; but what I do is the wrong which is against my will."

When such a carnal Christian confronts an unbeliever, it is not long before the Outsider sees in the life of this carnal Christian doubt, defeat, and discouragement. Mr. Christian is argumentative; he has a quick temper. His goals are self-centered, his purposes often unknown. He may be legalistic—full of "Thou Shalts" and "Thou Shalt Nots." He is prayerless. He is undisciplined. The Outsider cannot find the indwelling Christ in such a man! Give this Christian ten training courses and . . . it will not help him one bit! Nothing is going to change his sterile life-style except for him to discover the meaning of the Christ-filled life.

When Christians stop worrying about *Doing* and start showing concern about *Being*, there will be more and more Spirit-filled believers who understand the futility of attempting to serve Christ with "consecrated flesh." God does not need "consecrated flesh!"

Do you know how to spell the word "self"? Just take the word "flesh," take off the "h," and spell it backward—s-e-l-f. That's all "flesh" is!

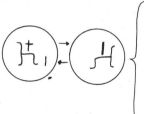

CONSISTENT LIFE

LOVE

JOY

PEACE

CONCERN FOR LOST

SELF-CONTROL

ACTIVE PRAYER LIFE

HUNGER FOR WORD

FORGIVING SPIRIT

CHRIST

REVEALED

IN

YOU!

Fig. 12, THE OUTSIDER MEETS A SPIRIT-FILLED BELIEVER

Most Christians today do not need training in methodology: we know more now than we can use or do. They need to be filled with the Spirit of God, to surrender their will to the will of God, to discover the meaning of a Christ-consistent life. Their lives need to reveal love, joy, peace, rivers of concern for the lost, self-control, an active prayer life, a hunger for the Word of God, and a forgiving spirit! These, of course, are the fruits of the Spirit—not the rewards of a study course.

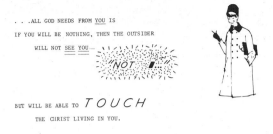

. . .ALL GOD NEEDS FROM YOU IS

IF YOU WILL BE NOTHING, THEN THE OUTSIDER

WILL NOT SEE YOU...

NOT

BUT WILL BE ABLE TO *TOUCH*

THE CHRIST LIVING IN YOU.

Fig. 13, THE BELIEVER IS NOW ENGAGED IN GOD'S WORK!

Outsiders will seek Christ's salvation as the result of a Christ-changed, Christ-revealing life. They will not be reached by well-rehearsed dialogue or a "perfect" new gospel tract. God uses *lives* to reveal His miracle-working power! A believer's life, owned and operated by Jesus Christ, is always God's raw material for effective evangelism. All He needs from us in order to win a lost world of Outsiders is NOTHING! We must quit trying to dedicate our gifts and talents and abilities, cease to pray, "Lord, I'm going to do something very beneficial for you." We must be willing to cry out, "Not I, but Christ!" Outsiders can TOUCH the Christ who lives in us when we permit Him to reveal Himself. Only then is the believer authentically engaged in God's work. He must simply become a *container for the Lord Jesus Christ.* That is really all the "program" God has.

Our emphasis must be on the being, the being, *the being,* and if the being is right, out of our innermost being will flow "rivers of living water!" A TOUCH ministry should not be something organized by a committee, but something structured by the Holy Spirit.

Consider the TOUCH ministry of John. John works for the FAA, in Air Traffic Control. After discovering what it meant to be totally yielded to Christ, he prayed, "Lord, what can You do through a man who works for FAA?" God said, "John, I want you to love sick children in hospitals, and let them discover my love for them." John said, "Lord, I don't know how to do that! I don't even know

how I would get into a hospital to share your love with them."
The Lord said, "I will show you the way."

One day soon after that, John met a clown. He received a thought inspired by his "resident boss." He bought a clown suit and had a professional clown teach him how to use makeup and how to wear the little bald-head piece and the big "feet" fifteen inches long. He began to blow up ballons, twisting them to make little animal dolls.

At present, John visits nearly all hospitals in San Antonio. Almost every day "Silly Willy" can be seen in the children's wards. He presents a special TOUCH tract which includes his picture as a clown and another of him in regular clothing. He writes to the youngsters when they go home from the hospital, often mailing them a little plastic gospel glove. Many children have found Christ through his ministry. All John had to do was yield his life totally to Christ, and the Within One began to love through him!

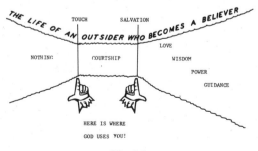

WHAT DOES THE CHRIST IN ME DO?

1. ASSIST IN SPIRITUAL GROWTH
   (THE "COURTSHIP" STAGE)
2. CONSTANT WITNESS – UNCONDITIONAL LOVE
3. HELP FRIEND BE AWARE OF NEGATIVE ATTITUDES
   AND GUIDE HIM TO POWER OF HOLY SPIRIT
4. ENCOURAGE FRIEND TO <u>TRUST</u> CHRIST AND <u>HIS</u> POWER TO OVERCOME
   PROBLEMS

THE LIFE OF AN OUTSIDER WHO BECOMES A BELIEVER

TOUCH   SALVATION

NOTHING   COURTSHIP   LOVE   WISDOM   POWER   GUIDANCE

HERE IS WHERE
GOD USES YOU!

Fig. 14

What can the Christ-in-me do for an Outsider? He assists in *developing spiritual insight* within the unbeliever. Consider the diagram just provided: the Outsider initially has no sensitivity to Christ within his life. He then meets a Christian who does more than knock on a door to invite him to come to church! This Christian begins a patient, consistent friendship—and Christ is revealed. The "courtship" now begins, through which spiritual understanding may occur, eventually leading to salvation. The Outsider's surrender to Christ changes him from the man who has a "dark chamber" in his life to a man who fully understands God's love, wisdom, power, and guidance.

Take Phil as an example. Phil is the owner of a carnival. His wife was a night club dancer who came to know Christ through another dancer who found Christ and witnessed to her. Phil thought his wife had "flipped her lid" when she became a Christian! He attended church services reluctantly, bitterly, and cynically. Nevertheless, Phil constantly TOUCHed the Christ who lived within Christians. Many of them invited him home for Sunday dinner, and a courtship began between Christ and Phil. After a few weeks Phil said, "You know, I can't get over these Christians. I've always thought all Christians were phonies, but these people are real!" He continued, "I'm not ready to receive Christ yet, but I'm not really anxious to turn Him away, either." A Christian friend said, "Phil, do you remember when you met your wife? You said to yourself, 'She's pretty! I think I'll date her.' You began to date, and there came a day when you said, 'I love that gal!' You may have kept it to yourself for awhile, but pretty soon you said, 'I can't live another day without her as my wife.' Finally there came the moment when you said, 'Honey, I love you! Let's get married.' " His friend continued, "Phil, that's where you are right now in your relationship with Christ. You have established contact with the Christ who lives inside your new Christian friends, and you are now falling in love with Jesus Christ. One of these days you will discover you can't live without him. When you do, you will be ready to surrender your life to Him." That conversation occurred on a Sunday afternoon; the following Wednesday night, Phil accepted Christ.

God uses Spirit-filled Christians in a unique way during the courtship stage, the period of initial spiritual awareness. He uses Christians to constantly witness of the indwelling Christ, who is revealed through simple fellowship. The Christian who always shows unconditional love will help his Outsider friend become aware of his negative attitudes concerning Jesus and will guide him toward the Cross by the power of the Holy Spirit. He then will be used to lead the Outsider to trust Christ's power to overcome all problems that may stand in the way of personal commitment.

Jesus Christ is the key that unlocks every problem in life!

If that statement is true, the only plan of evangelism Christians need is to reveal the indwelling Christ to Outsiders. Unbelievers can then discover his love and be converted.

There is no other way.

NOTES

1. See also Chapter 1 in my book, *Witness, Take the Stand*; entitled "Introducing 'Mr. Outsider,' " available from Evangelism Division, Baptist General Convention of Texas, 703 N. Ervay, Dallas, Texas 75201.

2. Dr. Hart's book, *Brick by Brick,* to be published soon, will be of invaluable assistance to the reader.

3. Numbers in parentheses in this chapter correspond to numbers on the diagram.

4. See page 45 in Dr. Grubb's marvelous book, *The Liberating Secret* (Fort Washington, Penn.: Christian Literature Crusade, 1955).

Chapter 5
The Spirit Uses Small Groups

When Christians minister, they must always remember that the "church" is not a building, bur rather part of the Family of God. Outsiders can be introduced to the "church" without ever setting foot in a sanctuary. The Family of God can minister, therefore, in any living room or around any kitchen table. Thousands of Outsiders can be reached from these small-group meetings in homes who would never attend formal religious services.

Short-term, impersonal, formal relationships with unbelievers frequently do not last long enough for the reality of Christ to be revealed. When TOUCH groups are formed, the relationship with unbelievers over a long period of time offsets these handicaps by a setting leading to deeper relationships.

1. How the Holy Spirit Can Use Groups

This chapter is designed to show how Christ can work through the "church" in small-group ministries, most of which take place in homes. Small groups are nothing new. Most Sunday School classes are small groups. In fact, Christians have been functioning in small groups for years. Nevertheless, the techniques [1] change radically when the small group meets in a home—with Outsiders comprising fifty per cent or more of those present.

TOUCH house-groups are being greatly used of the Lord in Spirit-filled evangelism. They allow opportunity for Christians to share, to listen, and to sense the "spiritual climate" within the Outsider's life.

2. Small Groups in TOUCH Ministries

The ways to use small groups in TOUCH ministries are countless. Here are a few examples: Guy and Evelyn are continually inviting small groups of Christians and Outsiders to share their Sunday dinner. Christians naturally communicate their faith as the meal progresses, and frequently Outsiders receive Christ. Included among them has been a striptease dancer who used the stage name "Sandy Sin." She became "Sandy Saved" on Sunday afternoon in Guy and Evelyn's living room.

Mildred uses a small group for her Neighborhood Bible Study. Her TOUCH ministry has grown so fast that she has had to divide the group, using both the dining room and the living room.

A TOUCH drug ministry uses small groups for sharing problems. The addicts meet three nights a week for sharing times. The not-yet converted meet in one group, the "baby Christians" in another group, with the more mature Christians in a third group. Each group is structured according to the needs of the participants.

3. The Three-Way Relationships in Small Groups

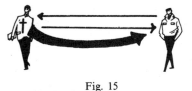

Fig. 15

A three-way relationship takes place whenever a believer and an Outsider begin to talk; the Christ who dwells within the believer is revealed to the unbeliever, and he recognizes that there is *something more* to this Christian's life than just body and soul. For this reason, it is not necessary always to be "preaching" to an Outsider in order to be sharing Christ with him. Small groups are a matter of *involvement,* and it is important that participants not be constantly looking for an opening to "convert" the Outsider. The involvement will break down the barriers, and the Spirit will direct the Christian to know His time for conversion.

People are not threatened as much by spiritual "gut-conversation" in a small group as they would be if the conversation were part of an "eyeball-to-eyeball" confrontation. Often a greater openness to serious conversation will be available in the small group than in a one-to-one relationship.

Listen for one of four ways the Holy Spirit may use to TOUCH an Outsider. Whether this group is a Bible study or one of the many ways a small group can be used for a TOUCH ministry, these are areas where the Holy Spirit may reach the Outsider.

```
THROUGH HIS NEED FOR, DESIRE FOR.
    I. Security
            Food, shelter, clothing not enough. . .
            Money not enough . . .

   II. New Experience
            Drugs, pleasure, lust - satisfactions,
            Ego builders not enough . . .

  III. Recognition
            A desire to "be somebody" in somebody's eyes
            But to feel ill at ease with God. . .something
                                               missing. . .

   IV. Response
            Feeling that others enjoy being with him. . .
            As a Christian, the Master-In-You reaches out. . .
            (You may hate sin, but Jesus loves sinners!)
```

Fig. 16

(1) *Through a need or desire for security.* Some people work themselves into a state of exhaustion trying to collect all the "goodies" of life and then discover it is not enough. When they make

that discovery, they will be open to the Spirit's voice.

(2) *Through a search for a new experience.* Teen-agers often are searching for a thrill—drugs, pleasure, lust, satisfactions. Adults often are trapped by "ego builders," constantly joining a new club and trying new hobbies. New experiences all become "old." The Holy Spirit can meet each person's need for security: salvation through Jesus Christ is the only really secure experience in the universe. Further, there is *no greater experience* than walking daily with Christ in control.

(3) *Through a thirst for recognition.* This manifests itself in a desire to "be somebody" in someone else's eyes. Such a person will always feel ill at ease with God and always be aware that something is missing.

(4) *Through a need for response from others.* Some individuals come into the small group feeling that others do not always enjoy being with them. They are lonely. I have met many wealthy women whose husbands are top-drawer executives; yet they live for tranquilizers and bridge games and are crying out for someone to love them. When they discover that Christ offers the greatest love in the world and that the greatest way to "be somebody" is to become a container for a living Master, the Holy Spirit utilizes these basic needs of the lost person to reveal the changes Christ can make in a life.

Christians may hate sin, but if they go beyond that to hate sinners, they cannot expect to be used of the Lord. We are always to hate the sin and love the sinner, regardless of how miserable, filthy-mouthed, drunk, immoral, lustful, or hateful that person might be. Christ in us is capable of loving the unlovable person!

4. Small Groups Must be Designed for Outsiders

The specific activity of the small group will not always be religious if Outsiders are to be TOUCHed. Herein lies a danger. Christianity today includes many carnal Christians who simply want to "do something for humanity." If the purpose of sharing Christ is not kept uppermost, TOUCH groups will not achieve their objective.

TOUCH groups can focus on many themes, including literacy

training. West Memorial Baptist Church is now helping foreign women read and write, using the Laubach method. As we teach them to read, we also communicate Christ's message. We do not wish to send them to the same Christless hell as literates to which they would go as illiterates. TOUCH ministries aim to provide activities through which we may share the indwelling, living Christ with an individual. I have visited churches which are teaching international women every week. Some of the classes have been functioning for five or more years and have not yet seen a dozen converts. Other churches doing exactly the same thing—with a different spiritual commitment within the hearts of the Christian women who teach—are seeing a half-dozen or more women converted every year. Our purpose as Christians is to *evangelize,* not socialize.

Some years ago we wanted to start a ministry in a huge high-rise apartment house in Philadelphia. Eight hundred families lived under one roof. They had practically every facility imaginable there. Residents could have their car repaired, have their teeth fixed, make bank deposits, or do their grocery shopping, and never leave the complex . . . but there was no witness for Christ in the building. We found we could not get past the doorkeeper into the lobby to share Christ. A Christian mother from North Carolina lived nearby. She was a gifted interior decorator. At her suggestion we started an interior decorating course in the Club Room of the apartment house. We charged $10.00 or $12.00 for the six-week course. The teacher was that committed Christian woman who had a master's degree in interior decorating. Her helpers just "happened" to be some of us who longed to see a witness develop in the complex. We discovered that many residents were young secretaries, two or three living in one plush apartment. They had no money for furnishings. They were shown how they could dye burlap and make fancy drapes and how they could buy old junk and antique it. Bit by bit we developed friendships in the apartment complex until we could finally walk up to that formidable doorman and say, "I want to see Miss Mary Smith." Miss Smith, who lived up on the twelfth floor, would be notified by the doorman that she had visitors in the lobby. She would walk over to her television set, turn it to the monitor channel, and recognize us standing in the lobby being photographed by a television camera. She would reply to the doorman, "Oh, please tell them to come up." Through those contacts we had the joy of seeing several Outsiders accept Christ. From that interior decorating class the University Baptist Chapel was begun in the YWCA in downtown Philadelphia, and it is still functioning.

5. Groups Must Begin at the Spiritual Level of the Outsiders

In working with hard-core Outsiders, it is important to *begin where they are* spiritually. We have experimented with a Bible study group for adults who are spiritual illiterates. We began by sending a letter to all those living in an apartment complex. It said:

Mark 1:8

If you are not sure what the two dots between the 1 and the 8 on the line above stand for, this letter is for you!

A good many men would sincerely like to understand the Scriptures better, but they are uneasy about attending a "traditional" Bible study. They are afriad they might be embarrassed by their lack of knowledge of the Bible, that they might be asked to read a verse aloud and be unable to pronounce the words of Bible characters or places, or that someone might assume they know more than they actually do about the Bible.

Have you ever thought in these terms?

If so, you are invited to a Bible Discussion Group which will begin Sunday morning, April 4, at 10:00 A.M., at 14725 Barryknoll, London Townhouse #116. This is:

1. a class for men
2. who do not have a great deal of Bible background,
3. who are interested in open-minded discussion.

Come dressed any way you please, with or without a copy of the New Testament (we'll provide one), and with the assurance that everyone else in the group will be sympathetic with your desire to learn.

This Bible study, which will be strictly non-doctrinal, is being initiated by a group of men who are interested in having a sharing time with people of any or no faith. Whether you now—or ever in the future—attend a church regularly will be considered a strictly personal matter and will not enter into the structure of this group of men.

Should the class grow larger, it may be divided. For now, there is room for you. For more information, call 497-0108.

We handpicked three or four men who could communicate effectively and would understand the importance of not embarrassing visitors by asking "information questions." These men were advised, "If the Outsider asks what 'Jas.' stands for, explain without even smiling that this is the abbreviation for the book of James. Then tell him that James is found in the New Testament and that the New Testament and the Old Testament are the two major divisions of the Bible. Stay with the basics." Such a class in a large city will grow simply because there are many people who have never been to church.

Some time ago I experimented with a small group which was simply called "The Atheists' Club." The members were met through continuous contact with Outsiders from other TOUCH ministries. The group was open to atheists who were searching for truth. I gave each person a copy of *Mere Christianity* by C. S. Lewis, and we simply discussed his comments about the Christian faith. Eventually these men began to include those who "boxed themselves into a corner," and several became believers. The problem of any atheist is always the problem of a proud "I" in the heart. The doubts are not always intellectual. Let atheists rattle around long enough about their doubts, provide thought-provoking questions here and there (the fewer the better), and after a while they will begin to realize that their real problem is rebellion against the Christ who demands full ownership of every man.

Why will an Outsider join a group? Some will join because of a *traditional interest in Bible study.* "When I was a little girl, I used to go to Sunday School for Bible study. This appeals to me."

Others will join because *friends belong.* Friendships draw more people into small groups than any other single factor. Others will join because of *loneliness*. Because there are so many lonely people today and because they will join small-group activities, it is valuable preparation for Christians working in TOUCH groups to read Earl Jabay's book, *Search for Identity*.[2] When Christians become sensitive to the conduct of frustrated people, they will find it much more rewarding to work with them. Finally, others will join because of interest in a *specific activity*—gardening, great books, Bible study, etc.

6. COMMUNICATION PATTERNS IN SMALL GROUPS

Communication patterns in small groups are very important. If you have one person talking to one person, you have two lines of communication. Add one more person, and you have six lines of communication. Add a fourth person, and there are twelve lines of communication. Gather a total of seven people, and you have forty-two different directions that conversation can occur.

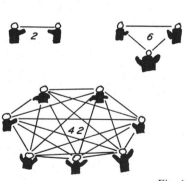

SEVEN OR EIGHT PEOPLE

ARE MAXIMUM FOR

EFFECTIVE WORK IN

A SMALL GROUP

Fig. 17

One can readily recognize that when the group includes more than eight people, the number of communication directions becomes astronomical. If there are more than eight people, it is wise to divide into subgroups. If this is not done, there will frequently be groups of three or four chatting together within the larger number. Large groups usually break up into these "chatter clusters" because people normally relate to each other in small units. For this reason, small-group TOUCH ministries are not encouraged to grow large. It is better to divide them, even between the living room and dining room of the same residence.

A. Leading a Small Group

Fig. 18

The best suggestion for leading a small group is: DON'T! Don't be the "leader"; don't have a teacher; you may not even need an "expert." Let the Lord work *through the entire group.* As a Christian, simply be a catalyst for the Holy Spirit to use in witnessing for Jesus. The most important thing the Christian can do in any small group for many weeks will be to *listen.*

There are four ways a Christian may function within a small group: as an *encourager*—warm, loving, listening to the ideas of others; as a *harmonizer*—helping to relieve conflicts; as a *gate keeper*—encouraging the silent to "open up"; and as one who is *seeking information*—developing a thought by asking questions like "Jane, explain more about that to me."

The Christian can function in one or more of these roles almost continually. Notice that none are ego-centered. The Christ in me will not try to exalt *my* ability or *my* knowledge, but will encourage, harmonize, "open the gate" for a shy person to share, or seek information. He will reveal His compassionate interest in the unbeliever through me.

B. Nonverbal Communication in a Small Group

Use your eyes to notice nonverbal communication: postures and facial reactions. The real value of the small group is not in trying to preach somebody into the kingdom of God, but in letting Jesus Christ live through your life, revealing Himself in the big or little statements made.

Posture, as well as facial and hand gestures, communicates as well as words. A posture of leaning backward in a chair is saying, "I'm through talking." Perhaps a person is sitting in the group, and suddenly you look at his hands. They are clenched into fists. That communicates! To be pushing a fingernail into the quick of one of the fingers on the opposite hand says something. What are people "saying" by their nonverbal actions? They may be saying, "I'm embarrassed," "I'm frustrated," or "I'm hurt." Posture, eyes, and hands all communicate. Those working in small groups need to be sensitive to these nonverbal signs.

Someone may come into the group and not say a word for a solid hour. *What is he saying?* To know, just watch posture and other nonverbal reactions. Sometimes it is obvious that you should let him alone. When he is ready, he will talk. Don't try to get everyone to answer everything and to commit themselves.

Have you ever noticed that there are some people who are so insecure that they have to try to convince the group of their importance by always making a comment about everything? The best way to handle that person is gently and with love.

C. Room Arrangements Communicate, Too!

One must be careful not to destroy the spirit of sharing in a small group. Here are some cautions concerning *room arrangements.* Do not set up the room with *lecture seating;* it engenders one-way conversation. Another problem to avoid is *space seating.* If a living room is set up with a couch on one wall, a pair of chairs in a far corner, and a chair here and a chair there with an end table between them, the long distances between chairs in the room will automatically foster subgroups. The three sitting on the couch will become a subgroup; the two in chairs in the corner will probably not know what to do and will either relate to each other or just feel lonely.

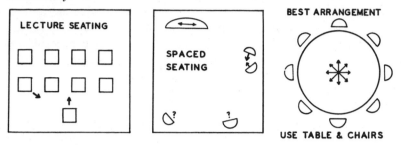

Fig. 19

The best possible arrangement for a small-group meeting is *around a table*. The mass of the table connects the bodies, and intimacy occurs as a result that cannot occur in any other type of setting. For this reason, as a pastor I have learned not to talk with a person about receiving Christ from across the wide expanse of a living room. I will often say, "Bill, I want to put my Bible on a table where we can read it together. Could we use the kitchen or dining room table?" In that setting we are seated close together. Physical proximity is a very important principle in small-group work.

D. Attitudes in Small Groups

There are a number of *attitudes* that can break down the sharing spirit in a small group. For example, there is the *dominator*—a person who just "takes over." There is the *blocker*—the individual who will always find reasons why a proposal won't work. Then there is the *anecdoter*—the character who constantly has to disturb the trend of conversation with a joke. Include the *play boy*—psychologically obsessive-compulsive, this person will sit in the group busily rolling up paper, doodling, or doing something else that detracts from the thought processes of the group. Include also the *recognition seeker*—a person who is always giving an opinion and trying to be recognized. One also meets the *special interest pleader*—"I belong to a certain club, and we are trying to do so and so, and I would like to tell you all about it."

These problems are best solved by having the group *adopt ground rules* at the first meeting. These ground rules should be agreed upon by the group, and they then become a basis upon which the offender may be gently reminded that he is "chasing rabbits." Because the group itself organizes and structures the ground rules, the leader is not considered to be unfair if a person needs to be guided into the real issue under discussion. (Ground rules for Witness training Groups, for example, have been provided on the inside cover of *Witness, Take the Stand!*).

E. Tips for Small Groups

Here are some tips for small groups, taken from the literature of the Neighborhood Bible Studies.

(1) Encourage discussion by asking several people to contribute answers to a question. "What do the rest of you think?" or "Is there anything else which could be added?" are ways of encouraging discussion.

(2) Be flexible and skip any questions which do not fit into the discussion as it progresses.

(3) Deal with irrelevant issues by suggesting again the purpose of your study. Suggest an informal chat about tangential or controversial issues after the regular study is dismissed.

(4) Receive all contributions warmly. Never bluntly reject what anyone says, even if you think the answer is incorrect. Instead, ask in a friendly manner, "Where did you find that?" or "Is that actually what it says?" or "What do some of the rest of you think?" Allow the group to handle problems together.

(5) Be sure you don't talk too much as the leader. Redirect those questions which are asked you. A discussion should move in the form of an asterisk, back and forth between members, not in the form of a fan, with the discussion always coming back to the leader. The leader is to act as moderator. As members of a group get to know each other better, the discussion will move more freely, progressing from the fan to the asterisk pattern.

(6) Don't be afriad of pauses or long silences. People need time to think. Never, *never* answer your own question—either use an alternate question or move on to another area for discussion.

(7) Watch hesitant members for an indication by facial expression or bodily posture that they have something to say, and then give them an encouraging nod or speak their names.

(8) Discourage too talkative members from monopolizing the discussion by specifically directing questions to others. If necessary, speak privately to the over-talkative one about the need for discussion rather than lecture in the group, and enlist his aid in encouraging all to participate.[3]

7. ICEBREAKERS FOR SMALL GROUPS

The best icebreaker available for a new group, whether it focuses upon interior decorating or Bible study, is the "Quaker Questions." After a few minutes of polite chatting, have the group (no more than eight) sit in a *close circle.* Suggest that the group get acquainted by using a set of four questions which originated within a Quaker community. Explain that they were used to get acquainted with a new Friends family. While they are not "nosey" questions, they help people know each other better.

Then present Question 1 (FROM MEMORY!), answer it yourself, and invite the person to your right to do the same. Each question is answered by all before the next question is presented.

Should there be more than eight in the group, divide into subgroups. Eight people, using two minutes per question, can complete the questions in about an hour. If you are serving refreshments, do so *before* you begin the questions.

Question 4 give each Christian ample *opportunity to witness!*

THE QUAKER QUESTIONS

1. **Where did you live between the ages of seven and twelve, and how many brothers and sisters were at home?**
2. **How did you heat your house?**
3. **Which person was the "warmest" person in your life?**
4. **When did God become more than a word to you?**

One of the best things I have found for Rap-Ins for teen-agers is to ask each one to answer the question, "Who loved you the most at a time when you were the least lovable?" Instant honesty occurs with teenagers when that question is used. One boy began such a group discussion by saying, "I guess it would be my dad the night I took his car without permission and wrecked it." Another boy told how he had come home intoxicated and how it broke his parents' hearts. Out of such openness and honesty, hungry beggars can be introduced to The One Who said, "I am the Bread of life."

8. The Goal of the Small Group: Find the "Hole in the Heart"

Our goal is to *find the hole in the Outsider's heart.* Nothing is any more important for a significant relationship than to find that hole! It can be a problem—a mother with a teen-age boy who is breaking her heart, a husband with a wife who is about to leave him, a man whose business is about to go bankrupt, or the couple who just discovered their little boy has cancer. Sooner or later everyone will have a gaping hole in his heart, and through that hole the good news of Jesus Christ can be shared as the power of God for salvation.

Sometimes a great amount of patience will be required to discover the hole in the heart. We do not share intimate things with people we do not know well. With those we love dearly and who dearly love us, we share our innermost concerns, burdens, and frustrations. After this intimacy develops, we will see Christ sharing His love through us. Then our witness (that is, telling the facts) can be borne. Then, when God moves within an Outsider's life, we encourage the courtship. We remain alert for the time when that individual will be ready to receive Christ.

Use after-group times for intimate, personal sharing. Many times an individual is embarrassed by our saying something personal to him or her in front of the group. Be alert for the ways God is working during group sessions, and help the atmosphere move toward God by little comments and truths shared.

Remember, evangelism is *one hungry beggar telling another hungry beggar where to find bread.*

THE OUTSIDER
FINDS IT HARD
TO BELIEVE YOU
WANT HER TO BE
IN HEAVEN UNTIL YOU HAVE HER IN YOUR HOME!

Fig. 20

Most important of all, the Outsider finds it hard to believe you want him to be with you in heaven *unless you want him in your home.* Whenever believers become involved with Outsiders to the extent that Christ reveals Himself, lives explode with awareness that when He is lifted up He draws all men to Himself.

NOTES

1. People often confuse the use of the words "dynamics" and "techniques." All groups have inter-action, called *dynamics. Techniques,* however, are such things as the "Quaker Questions." One cannot "use" *dynamics*—they *are.* One uses *techniques.* A good discussion of this matter is found in Clyde Reid's *Groups Alive—Church Alive* (New York: Harper and Row, 1969).

2. Earl Jabay, *Search for Identity* (Grand Rapids: Zondervan Press, 1967).

3. Marilyn Kunz and Catherine Schell, *The Acts of the Apostles: 18 Discussions for Group Bible Study* (Dobbs Ferry, New York: Neighborhood Bible Studies, 1969), p. 5.

Chapter 6
Spirit-Filled Communication

For the words that the mouth utters come from the overflowing of the heart. A good man produces good from the store of good within himself (Matt. 12:34-35).

Spirit-filled evangelism must be focused upon the Christ who is the real Source of Life. There are certain principles involved in communication with Outsiders which are both biblical and practical, and high pressure is not one of them!

Consider the dictionary definition of the word "communicate": to impart, participate, transfer, transmit, join, connect, make common to all what one presently possesses. The first definition of communicate is the word "impart": the dictionary defines this word as "causing another or others to have what is primarily one's own." Spirit-filled evangelism will concentrate on *causing someone else to have what is primarily your own.*

For instance, in your opinion, is this statement true or false?

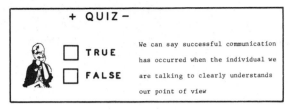

Fig. 21

That statement is false!

When we understand the meaning of the word "impart," we realize that communication does not occur until we "cause another to have what is primarily one's own." Evangelistic communication is not simply a matter of helping the Outsider *understand* Christ's redemption; it is a matter of his *receiving* it!

Authentic evangelism always involves imparting something which is *primarily one's own*. Only a Spirit-filled Christian can share "from the store of good within himself." The reason there are so many immature Christians in today's churches is because we have so many immature concepts concerning the true nature of evangelism. *We cannot lead a person beyond where we ourselves are.* The power of Billy Graham's ministry does not rest on personal "magnetic charisma," but rather his totally yielded life! One cannot miss the shining of Christ through him, whether he is on a platform before throngs, or conversing with him personally!

There are two levels of communication, broadly used in discussions of semantics in general education. Sometime ago, in listening to Dr. Clyde Fant of Southwestern Baptist Theological Seminary speak about these matters, an applied use of these concepts to the field of Spirit-filled evangelism seemed obvious.

The first level is *phatic* communion. Dr. Fant calls this "hello" communication. Liddell & Scott's *Greek-English Lexicon* describes the Greek word *phatos* as meaning something "said, spoken, that may be spoken, uttered, or named," from which we receive the English word "emphasis," meaning "the force of an expression which means more than meets the ear."

Phatic communion is a form of *pre-evangelism*. It is necessary to create a sense of mutual acceptance, of meeting another person on the plane of the senses. In phatic communion we are containing and communicating the expanding, redeeming power of the Holy Spirit, which is far, far more than that "which meets the ear."

The Christian develops a spirit of mutual acceptance in phatic communion. He says, "I'm here and you're there. I accept the fact that you are there, and you are accepting the fact that I am here." This can take two minutes at a gas station where a close relationship begins to develop at once with the attendant, or it can take a much longer time with a person who has been hurt in the past by someone who "looked like you." There will be a delay with one who dislikes you because you have a voice "like Mother's" or because you have the wrong kind of drawl. Phatic communion must occur before you can share impact ("brass tacks") communion. Many times Christians move into sharing Christ too fast and scare the Outsider away from a deep personal friendship.

I always cringe a bit when I see one who walks up to a stranger and says, "Hello, brother! If you died right now, would you go to hell?" Occasionally, such an approach may find someone who is so under conviction that he will reply, "Let's talk about it," but 90 percent of the time that approach is much too fast, and the person avoids further friendship or conversation. In working with Outsiders, phatic communion is really necessary.

Impact communion, however, is "brass tacks" communication. As Dr. Fant explained, this involves two things: *predictability* and *distance.* That is, when somebody knows exactly what language you are going to use and what conclusions you are going to reach, the impact is zero. The trouble with many Christians who talk to unbelievers rests in their predictability. They begin to talk about the Lord, their eyeballs roll up, and they use all the "starry words" like "saved," "lost," "blessed," "beautiful," etc. The unbeliever thinks, "Oh, dear! Here we go again! I've heard this religious vocabulary ever since I was a kid." All his defense mechanisms shoot up because there is nothing fresh or new being said.

A great problem beyond predictability is *distance.* How close to the Outsider's situation or need is the topic of the conversation?

If we talk to a man who is dying of cancer about heaven, that may be important. However, he may be far more concerned about who will support his family when he is dead. If you talk to an eight-year-old boy about heaven, he may be much more interested in the fact that Pop is a drunk and home is hell-on-earth. Heaven may not be the uppermost problem in his life right now; it may be his home life! We must be sure that *predictability* and *distance* are both considered in the kind of communication that we do.

Some years ago an Alaskan pastor walked up to Ted, one of the hell-raisingest, drinkingest, baudiest, most lecherous men in the Air Force. Introduced by a mutual friend, they shook hands on a street corner. The pastor said, "Ted, are you a Christian?"

Ted said, "Nope."

The pastor said, "Do you know how to be a Christian?"

Ted said, "Yep."

The pastor said, "Then you are a fool!" and turned on his heel and walked off.

That's *impact* communion!

Later Ted told me he was miserable for the rest of that day. He did not know whether to whip that preacher or to agree with him. That night he went to a service being conducted by the pastor. Ted was still miserable. He finally stood up in the middle of the sermon and said, "Why don't you give the invitation? I want to become a Christian!" He was converted. Impact communion had broken through his hardened condition.

Frequently, our communication problems stem from our being so crusted over with yesterday's language and attitudes that we cannot make an impact. While restructuring your thinking about this matter, remember this: *one step above impact is shock.* When a person goes into shock, either physically or spiritually, it is dangerous. What the Alaskan pastor said to Ted could not have been said by Ralph Neighbour. Not having the pastor's personality, my use of such impact would have been the end of my relationship with Ted.

This is one reason why there are no "canned approaches" in Spirit-filled evangelism. It is critically imperative to be led by the Holy

Spirit. He alone can be our Guide; He came for this purpose. "When your advocate has come, He will bear witness of me, and you also are my witnesses because you have been with me from the first" (John 15:26-27).

After phatic communion, we move into *impact communion,* in which the Holy Spirit directs our words. This Divine Flow in communication is all-important. Christ cannot flow into Outsider's lives until He has first come to rule in our lives. He flows freely only when I am wholly available to Him for His purpose.

THE DIVINE FLOW IN COMMUNICATION...

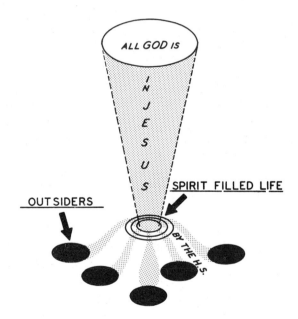

...RIVERS OF LIVING WATER!

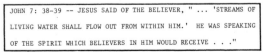

JOHN 7: 38-39 -- JESUS SAID OF THE BELIEVER, " ... 'STREAMS OF LIVING WATER SHALL FLOW OUT FROM WITHIN HIM.' HE WAS SPEAKING OF THE SPIRIT WHICH BELIEVERS IN HIM WOULD RECEIVE . . ."

Fig. 22

In Colossians we are told that "the fulness of the Godhead [that is, all God is] has come to dwell bodily in Jesus." Imagine! All that God is, is in Jesus. Is Jesus also in the Father? He said, "I and the Father are one." If you have seen me, you have seen the Father." Jesus *is* in the Father, and the Father *is* in the Son. Is the Spirit of God in Jesus? John tells us that Jesus "breathed upon them and gave them His Spirit." Yes, the Spirit of God is in Jesus. In Romans 8 we discover the fantastic truth which was described in an earlier chapter of this book: the "Sprit of God" is the "Spirit of Christ" who is the "Spirit of the One who raised Christ from the dead" who is the "Holy Spirit."

In Jesus I have the *fulness of God* as Father, as Son, and as Spirit. But He is more: He also became the *fulness of humanity.* He was tempted in all points as we are tempted. We may now add something to the essence of God the Father, Son, and Spirit in Jesus which is very important to us: Jesus was complete humanity. In His humanity *He also suffered death,* and He added the experience of death to all He was. He then add His *triumphant resurrection* to all He contained, and then He further included *His glorious ascension.* When He ascended to the right hand of the Father, He became *King of kings and Lord of Lords!*

Think of it! This One who is God the Father, Son, and Spirit, who has experienced in His incarnation humanity, death, and resurrection, who has ascended to the Father as both mediator and King of kings: *this very same Jesus has now come to dwell within us!* My communication with the Outsider flows from His divine presence in my life. As a Christian, I contain not only the fulness of the Godhead, but the fulness of His humanity, as His Spirit dwells within my spirit. He has been tempted in every point as I am tempted, yet without sin. What a resource for me to have for sharing the gospel with Outsiders! How awesome it is to grasp the full meaning of Jesus when He said to the believer, "Streams of living water shall flow out from within him" (John 7:38).

Speaking in tongues or an experience-centered "baptism into the Holy Spirit" [1] cannot communicate one fiftieth of the impact which is implicit in the truth that Christ dwells in the believer to communicate *through him* with the world about him. While I was baptized by the Holy Spirit the moment I accepted Jesus into my life, there was no guarantee that all of me would be under the continual supervision of the Holy Spirit. That precious Spirit cannot communicate Christ through me until I settle the fact that "I" have been crucified and have no need to flaunt who "I" am. The best protection against a breakout of tongues with a congregation is not to fight the wildfire, but to present the fire of the truth. When we understand the truth of Christ's fulness dwelling within the believer, we are not going to be drawn aside by half-truths.

SUMMARY OF COMMUNICATION STYLES

THE SHARING COMMUNICATION

* Encourages two-way communication

* Strives for joint understanding of problems and goals

* Willing to contribute ideas, suggestions

* Doesn't assume he's right

* Looks for new approaches

* Encourages exploration and experimentation

THE RULING COMMUNICATION

* Relies heavily on one-way communication

* Assumes that his own ideas and approaches are best

* Tries to impose or sell his own point of view

* Does not like to consider alternatives

* Is not interested in experimentation

THE GIVE-IN COMMUNICATION

* Shifts the burden to the other fellow

* Assumes the other fellow has more to contribute than he does

* Makes few contributions of his own ideas

* Willing to consider alternatives but doesn't work to develop them

* Willing to let others experiment

* Explores only to fit in with the other fellow's viewpoint

THE SPLIT COMMUNICATION

* Avoids interaction

* Assumes "nothing can be done"

* Neither contributes nor solicits contributions

* Not interested in new approaches

* Not interested in experimentation

* Emotionally-colored reactions

* No longer sensitive to the real issue

Fig. 23

The indwelling Christ becomes a river, a stream of living water, and that stream flows in love and joy. The words of a song say it beautifully: "There's peace like a river, joy like a river, and live like a river in my soul." That is so true! Spirit-filled evangelism is the communication that will share Jesus Christ with the world.

When pastors begin to preach *being* instead of *doing,* and when Christians discover the meaning and reality of the crucified life, then we will begin to see God's communication flowing through His church. Until then, there is no hope for us. There is no substitute. We will continue in our present carnal dog-trot of meetings and programs.

Consider the summary of communication styles in the above diagram. Our relationship to others can be one of *sharing, ruling, giving in,* or *splitting* from them. The Spirit-filled level of communication is *sharing.* A two-way relationship is established. There is a striving for joint understanding of needs and concepts. The Christian is willing to contribute ideas and suggestions, but he does not assume the stance of "Holy Man." The Christian looks for the opening given by the Spirit and encourages exploration and fellowship. There is a premissiveness in sharing in which there is acknowledgement that "we are all hungry beggars; some have not yet found the Bread."

What shall we say of the pathetic person who evangelizes through *ruling* or through one-way communication? I have often gone visiting with believers and suggested, "You lead our fellowship at this next house." Again and again my friend would smother any two-way conversation by a run-on monologue. It was as though he was saying, "I'm scared to stop. If you ask me anything, you might see how empty I really am." Ruling communication does not work! We must not assume that our own ideas and approaches are best and that the other person is wrong. We must not try to impose or sell our point of view. We should not refuse to let the Outsider consider other alternatives.

Sometime ago I talked with a long-hair in the Haight-Ashbury district of San Francisco. If I had started our relationship by trying to tell him about Christ, I would have failed before I started. Instead

I said, "Are you religious?"

"Yeah, man!"

"What kind of religion do you have?"

I'm a Buddhist."

"What type of Buddhist are you?"

"Well, I'm a Zen Buddhist."

"Tell me about that. I would like to know about a Zen Buddhist."

For thirty minutes we sat in the "Drugstore," and I let him tell me all about Zen. I *asked* question after question and *listened* to everything he said.

When he finished, I said, "That is very interesting."

Then he asked, "Are you a Buddhist?"

I said, "No, I'm a Christian."

"Oh!" he replied. "Uh, what kind of Christian are you?"

I said, "Oh, I don't know if you really are interested enough to want to know about it."

"Yeah, man, I do!" he enthusiastically said.

"Are you really sure? Do you have an hour to sit and talk?"

"Right on!"

By this time he was begging me to tell him about Jesus! I continued to use *sharing* communication. For one hour he asked questions. Had I tried to rule, we would not have had a five-minute friendship.

Another pattern in evangelism is *give-in* communication. In this situation the burden is shifted to the other person. One person assumes the other has more to contribute than he does, so he makes few contributions of his own ideas. He may be willing to consider alternatives plans, but he will not share in developing them because he was not given a share in making them.

In past months our Family of God in the experimental West Memorial Baptist Church has shared in preparing our goals, our covenant,[2] and the strategy for TOUCH. The members are deeply committed to a life-style. When I have shared our concepts with pastors and businessmen, they often have said, "My, that concept of the church is tremendous. I'm glad somebody is doing it. I don't think I could do it, but I'm glad you are." The difference is in the communication pattern! Our members have developed our life-style *together*. Those I tell about it have not shared in our months of joy and pain, and so their reaction is to "let us do

THE HUMAN FLOW IN COMMUNICATION

INFORMING **WE SHARE** **EXPLORING**

Let's consider this possibility . . .

Here's an additional thought . . .

I recently read . . .

Perhaps this might help . . .

What do you think about . . .

How long have you felt . . .

I'd like to understand . . .

Tell me about your spiritual pilgrimage.

I RULE
PERSUADING

I really feel I am right . . .

You really should go along . . .

It's absolutely necessary for you to . . .

You should not delay to . . .

DEMANDING

Hell is ahead, unless you . . .

If you don't do this, the results will be . . .

I must insist that you realize the consequences if . . .

I GIVE IN
ACCOMMODATING

Let's try it your way . . .

If you really feel that's best . . .

I'll trust your opinions . . .

COMPLYING

I'm not in agreement, but . . .

I don't want to stick my neck out . . .

I'll do it to solve a problem . . .

The only way to get along is to go along . . .

FIGHTING **WE SPLIT!** **FLIGHTING**

I have forgotten the problem. I'm now angry with you . . .

This has become personal now . . .

Who do you think you are, anyhow? . .

You have no right to . . .

Let me get away from this . . .

I'm too involved to see you . . .

I'd like to drop it, if you please . . .

There's no use in our talking more . . .

Fig. 24

it." For this very reason Spirit-filled communication with Outsiders must not be a "let-me-tell-you" event.

The final communication pattern is *splitting*. Interaction is avoided. Those communicating decide nothing can be said that will make any difference. Neither person contributes nor solicits contributions. Neither person is interested in a new approach, nor is there further interest in experimentation. Sadly, many relationships with unbelievers terminate by no further communication being possible. Self gets in the way in the Christian's witness, and Christ is not allowed to love the unbeliever. The relationship is prematurely terminated.

The diagram (Fig. 24) shows the various possibilities in verbal communication, adapted from often-used college lectures on this subject. Its particular application in this chapter is to Spirit-filled evangelism.

When we examine the record of our Lord conversing with the Samaritan woman in John 4:7-26, we find the following conversation. As a discipline of learning, use the diagram to determine which pattern of communication was used in each sentence:

CONVERSATION		PATTERN
JESUS:	Give me a drink.	_____
WOMAN:	What! You, a Jew, ask a drink of me, a Samaritan woman?	_____
JESUS:	If only you knew what God gives, and who it is that is asking you for a drink, you would have asked him and he would have given you living water.	_____

WOMAN: Sir, you have no bucket and this well is deep. How can you give me "living water"? Are you a greater man than Jacob our ancestor, who gave us the well, and drank from it himself . . .?

_____

JESUS: Everyone who drinks this water will be thirsty again, but whoever drinks the water that I shall give him will never suffer thirst any more. The water that I give him will be an inner spring always welling up for eternal life.

_____

WOMAN: Sir, give me that water, and then I shall not be thirsty, nor have to come all the way to draw.

_____

JESUS: Go home, call your husband, and come back.

_____

WOMAN: I have no husband.

_____

JESUS: You are right in saying that you have no husband, for, although you have had five husbands, the man with whom you are now living is not your husband; you told me the truth there.

_____

WOMAN: Sir, I can see that you are a prophet. Our fathers worshiped on this mountain, but you Jews say that the temple where God should be worshiped is in Jerusalem.

_____

JESUS: Believe me, the time is coming when you will worship the Father neither on this mountain, nor in Jerusalem. You Samaritans worship without knowing what you worship, while we worship what we know.

It is from the Jews that salvation comes. But the time approaches, indeed it is already here, when those who are real worshipers will worship the Father in spirit and in truth. Such are the worshipers whom the Father wants. God is spirit, and those who worship him must worship in spirit and in truth.   _____

WOMAN: I know that Messiah (that is Christ) is coming. When he comes he will tell us everything.   _____

JESUS: I am he, I who am speaking to you now.   _____

Note this important principle: He never permitted the conversation to drop onto the level of demand-comply or fight-flight. The crucial moment came when He probed into her guilt by referring to her promiscuity. She retaliated by quickly changing the subject—*and Jesus followed where she led the conversation.* He knew that the subject of her sin was too painful to be pursued, and she knew by his next comment that, *while He rejected her sin, He had not rejected her.* Notice also that our Lord did not attempt to "get a notch on His gun" by crowding her to believe. The record of the event makes no hint that she had become a believer—only a seeker (John 4:29).

It is important to virtually *memorize* the possibilities in conversation and to be aware that God works best in the freedom of love. Love never coerces; rather, it draws the other with its unmistakable resource of compassion. The Christ who dwells in us needs only our willingness to utilize God-controlled patterns of communication to use us to the fullest!

Notes

1. Merrill F. Unger stated in *The Baptizing Work of the Holy Spirit* (Wheaton, Ill.: Van Kampen Press, 1953), p. 79: ". . . it is explicitly stated that believers are 'baptized into one body' (1 Cor. 12:13). The declaration is definite that the Spirit is the Baptizer, and the Body of Christ is that into which He baptizes. Hence, it is proper to say 'baptism *with* the Spirit' or 'baptism *by* the Spirit,' but not baptism *in*, or *into*, the Spirit."

2. See Appendix for a copy of the Covenant.

Chapter 7
Pre-Evangelism

All great movements in evangelism have occurred in the context of an atmosphere in which men are sensitive to the presence of God. In today's culture, a secular man may live for years without being TOUCHed by a Christ-permeated climate. The harvest we now reap is primarily composed of converts from the church-related society.

The deadliest danger in the evangelism of the next quarter-century could be the hesitancy of churches to do anything about this matter! As the population doubles, it does not follow that the church-related society can be expected to double. We seem to be following the pattern of England, where each generation becomes increasingly godless. Nevertheless, the church-related population will show some increase each year simply because the total population is on its way to *doubling*. Today's hundred million religionists could grow to one hundred fifty million. Converts from this church-related population could provide a resulting statistical "church growth" which would hide the fact that we are not even *touching* the two hundred fifty million secularized people who ignore the church!

Such irrelevant "success reports" from churches are already lulling us to deadly sleep. A Baptist state convention recently recorded the "highest number of baptisms in history, finally exceeding a 'high' reached in the 1950's." This, it was concluded, demonstrates the churches are "excelling in evangelism." No attention was given by the analysis to the corresponding population growth over the past fifteen years in that state, with a resulting decrease in percentage of baptisms-to-total-population.

The truth is, today's *Christians have precious little contact with the Outsider world.* Few believers can honestly report as many as five intimate friends who are unbelievers. Insulated and isolated, we sing our anthems, raise our budgets, hear our sermons preached, and teach the Bible to our children—all in the snug security of a building unscripturally called "The Church"—while the exploding pagan population pass us on their way to cottages, beaches, and lakes . . . and hell!

There is absolutely no hope of changing this situation *apart from God's children accepting their role as ministers of the gospel.*[1] Only then can our nation feel again the *atmosphere* we desperately need in which men become sensitized to the presence of God. It borders on the level of an indictment for us to observe our nation becoming pagan at the present rate, while it still contains such a high percentage of Church-related people! We outstrip ancient Israel in terms of being "God's spoiled brat," selfishly hoarding our Good News for our children to hear, refusing to share our gospel with Outsiders.

Outsiders will not come to us. We must go to them. Our culture no longer automatically expresses Christianity. Our churches are no longer regarded as a *moral* voice and certainly are not respected as a *spiritual* voice. George Morris has written, "We are in a post-Christendom era while the population is pre-Christian, because it has never been Christian at all."[2]

The climate of awareness must be created in our urban centers, where godlessness and the population are greatest. *Developing this climate of awareness is called Pre-evangelism.* One college friend of mine defined Pre-evangelism as "Christ in me, loving the 'hell' out of people." He made a point! A man without Christ is filled with an eternal agony, separated from God. That kind of life *is hell,* whether it is before or after death. Pre-evangelism relates Christians to Outsiders on a one-to-one basis for a lengthy period of time to provide opportunity for Christ to reveal His undying love for all.

Pre-evangelism takes time, a commodity our generation heavily rations where evangelism is concerned. Most Christians find it easier to give *dollars* than *hours* to their Lord. The hours given are often dissipated in *good* activities, which limit the balance of time available for the *right* activity. It is precisely for this reason that "The People Who Care" in Houston have no choir. Although several members have college degrees in music, West Memorial Baptist Church has thus far decided it is bad stewardship to spend one full night each week rehearsing a five-minute selection for a worship service. There are simply too many bleeding hearts around us to be cared for!

Pre-evangelism requires authentic love for a person, and you cannot love in ten-minute segments as a part of Thursday's "visitation program." When one does offer love to an Outsider who does not wish to accept it, the deepest level of Christianity is plumbed by the Christian. That friendship must continue until the Outsider is ready to seriously consider Christ's claim to become Lord of his life. We must be patient enough to allow each person to come to Christ according to a Divine Timetable.

Moreover, this *Pre-evangelism must occur at a level which is not threatening to unbelievers.* That is, I cannot expect impact communion when only phatic communion is possible. The Christian must discipline himself to move more gradually into a deeper relationship with the unbeliever, or the opportunity to share Christ will be destroyed.

Pre-evangelism requires a TOUCH point.

Someone has said, "Only in the midst of the world is Christ, *Christ.*" The name "Christ" literally means "Savior." It is in the middle of our world that the Son of God becomes, in all of His power, a redemptive force. We have reached that time in the life of the Christian church where we must acknowledge the fact that we must expose Christ to the world, or we will die! Those who are insulated by the presence of the Holy Spirit in their lives do not have to be isolated from the sinful, dirty, old world! The Christian faith suffers violence not from lack of power, but from lack of *exposure*.

I well remember a certain town where I conducted a week of preaching services. They were held in a church where virtually every member had gone into spiritual retirement. The town, however, was alive . . . with lost people. The main highway cut the town in half and was lined by a long string of bars from one city limit sign to the other. I preached on Sunday, Monday, and Tuesday nights, and each service was packed with a huge crowd of eleven or twelve people, most of whom who slept through my sermons.

One of the deacons, however, was a deeply committed Christian. At dinner one night, the pastor, the education director, the deacon, and I decided to go after the Outsiders. The deacon and I chose to visit the beer joints on the south side of this street, and the pastor and education director were to visit those on the north side. We would go out after the service and visit every bar in town. We decided we would first walk up to the owner of the bar, shake hands, and tell him our names. Then we would find out his or her name and say, "I know something about you that you may not know about yourself, and it is wonderful!" We expected them to say, "What's that?" We would reply, "Jesus loves you." We agreed to look them square in the eye when we said it and not even blink.

The deacon's eyes began to twinkle; he said, "What will happen?"

I said, "All we need to do then is to *listen*." I explained that others had witnessed like this with me and nearly always the owners would begin to tell us how they felt about the Lord Jesus.

We all agreed to try it. After the next preaching service, we had a word of prayer and went to visit the bars.

The deacon and I had a whale of a time! We had more fun that night than we would have had at a circus. We shared Christ with a man who was sitting in a booth with someone else's wife. He was scared to death that he would be caught, and he went home. Next, we talked to a lovely Italian woman who ran one of the bars. She invited us into a little living room behind the bar, introduced us to her grandchildren, and asked us to pray with her. In another bar, we led a young man to Christ.

We returned to the church office at midnight to meet the other team for a report. When we got back, the pastor and education director were sitting in a car in the driveway. We all went into the office, and I let the deacon share our experiences. He was bubbling over with excitement: God had worked! Then I said, "Pastor, how did it go with you?"

He said, "Well, I'll tell you. When we drove up to that first bar, we sat out in front of it and thought what it might look like if the pastor and education director went into a beer joint. We decided that we did not want to have anyone say anything about us that might get us into hot water; so we came back, and we have been waiting for you ever since you left at 9:00 P.M."

I wish you could have seen the look of disappointment on that dear deacon's face!

It is time for us to acknowledge the fact that Christians do not have to be isolated from the sinful world! Jesus was a friend of winebibbers and sinners. It was a prostitute who bathed his feet with her ointment. Our Lord was a man who was notorious for being a friend to the ungodly.

Christians do not have to get dirty in the world. I have visited dozens of bars, and I have never yet ordered a beer in one of them. If I possibly can, I go whenever I am invited to a cocktail party: that is where the Outsiders are.

Some months ago I attended a group-psychotherapy convention with a member of my church, a physician who is a deeply committed Christian. I was invited to attend the cocktail party which followed. When we walked in, my friend said, "You meet those standing in the north half of the room, and I'll do the same in the south half. We'll ask the Lord to let us share Him here."

I chatted with eight or nine psychiatrists standing in a little circle at my end of the room. There were multiple opportunities to share Christ's message; indeed, some were hungry to discuss it with me. (Psychiatrists have a suicide rate six times greater than the national average!) What a mission field my dear doctor friend has . . . *at cocktail parties!* Possessing every credential other physicians possess, she cannot be "written off" as an illiterate.

There are scores of ways we can climatize this world to become aware of the gospel of Jesus Christ, but we must decide once and for all that we will no longer hide behind stained glass walls in order to protect ourselves. When we are ready to accept our mission and our mission field, there will be no limit to the TOUCH of the Spirit.

Two Christian men visited a house of prostitution, located in a beautifully decorated one hundred thousand dollar home (discovered by riding "shotgun" with the vice squad for a couple of nights). They found themselves in a huge living room, with fifteen or twenty men sitting around. They sat down beside one young man and began to share Christ with him. It turned out that he had been miserable for days and was groping for reality in a life which was dissipated and self-centered. He made a decision right there in the living room. On the following Sunday, he attended the worship service with his new friends, and today he actively shares in the ministry of that flock.

While that type of invasion of the devil's premises may not become commonplace among Christians, it does prove a point: *Christ does not need a holy environment to call unbelievers to repentance. God can work anywhere! Pre-evangelism finds the Outsider's "field of consciousness."*

In Mark 8:18 Jesus said, "Are your minds closed? You have eyes: Can you not see? You have ears: Can you not hear?" Christians who begin to relate to an Outsider must be aware that he does not always have the same "field of consciousness" as a church-oriented person. Because we see a thing, do we always "see" it? Because we hear a noise, do we always "hear" it? In the normal course of life, we often find examples which make us answer no to these questions. I hear a baby cry; the mother "hears" a call for a bottle or a declaration that it is diaper-changing time. Because of their close relationship, the mother and baby "hear" things from each other that a stranger would not catch.

In a recent committee meeting, one of the men had his mind locked into a problem other than the one under discussion. His "field of consciousness" was irrelevant to that of the other committee members. We finally stopped him and said, "Wait! You're talking about a completely different situation than we are talking about." He said, "Oh!" For ten minutes we had been out of "contact" with him.

In spiritual matters, it is often true that the Outsider's "field of consciousness" makes it difficult for us to share Christ at all. When working with the Outsider, it is important to recognize that the human mind is designed to blot out painful memories and serious faults. An unregenerate man may instinctively blot out the knowledge of deep sin and suffering within his own life. Many times the Christian can see clearly what the Outsider cannot recognize. We may think, "How can you *live* so wickedly? You've been cheating on your wife, you are stealing through your business practices, and you won't even admit you are a sinner! You tell me you are 'as good as the hypocrites in the church!' How blind can you be?" We then unconsciously feel disgust.

And rightly so, but that attitude will not help! It will not win that man to Christ, for Christ cannot use that attitude in us. *We need to realize that sin in a man's life is something that is revealed to him by the Holy* Spirit! Jesus said, "When he comes, He will . . . show where wrong and right and judgement lie. He will convict them of wrong, by their refusal to believe in me; he will convince them that right is on my side, . . . by showing that the Prince of this world stands condemned" (John 16:8-11).

Go back through that Scripture passage and underline every one of the "he's." We must be aware of the fact that *He* will convict of wrong, that *He* will convince them that right is on Jesus's side, and that *He* will convince them of divine judgement. That is *not our job!* When we try to do this work, we fail. We send the Outsider into the communication pattern of *flight* or *fight*. He will not enjoy our attempts to convince him he is a sinner. If he does not yet *acknowledge* himself to be a sinner, we seek to love him on that level.

Our task as Christians is to reveal the Christ who dwells in us. If we do that effectively, the Holy Spirit will do the convicting and convincing. In my own personal ministry, I need *never* deliberately set out to make people realize they are sinful, or that right is on the side of Jesus, or that they are facing a divine judgment. *That is the work of the Holy Spirit.* He uses me merely to reveal Jesus Christ as Lord. This too is done through the Holy Spirit, as I simply accept the honor of revealing the Lord Jesus.

During pre-evangelism, the believer may just be getting acquainted with the Outsider. Suppose they meet at a tavern. Chances are, the Outsider's "field of reference" sees nothing wrong with having a beer. He orders it with a clear conscience. He does not know that there is anything harmful in beer-drinking. If the Christian attempts a temperance lecture, it may well be the end of the friendship.

THINGS TO REMEMBER ABOUT PRE-EVANGELISM:

1. *Nearly everything a person does is based upon how he truly feels about himself.* Because a man is successful, it does not follow that he will always feel he is a success. He may be working twenty hours a day simply because he feels he is a failure. He may have more money than everyone else in town, but he may *feel* he is a pauper. In pre-evangelism, we must ask, "How does this person feel about himself?"

2. *Effective sharing of the gospel depends on the Holy Spirit, not YOU!* That not only takes a heavy load off your shoulders, but it gives you the freedom to be a channel, rather than to try to dig one. It is precisely in such freedom that Jesus reveals His life living in you.

3. *Every Outsider is interested in himself, not Jesus.* We must begin with what an Outsider is interested in. So we start with him.

If he likes to fish, we may fish together. If he likes to work in the garden, we will take an interest in his garden.

I recall one man who claimed not to believe in God. He had attended church only one since he married. According to his wife, the reason he came that Easter Sunday was because of two or three men who kept dropping by to chat with him about gardening. You see, his yard was his life! The men were interested in what he was interested in. Their Christian involvement was pre-evangelism. Sooner or later, this man may fall in love with the Christ living in his friends, and there may be a time when he will be converted.

4. *Learn to love the Outsider for what he will become.* What he is may be most unlovable to you. Think of what he can become if Christ enters his life!

A man here in Houston was a hard-core heroin user; his wife, a prostitute, was also on "smack." Since middle adolescence, the young man had been a burglar, except for a two and a half-year imprisonment. He struggled with the problem of his addiction and his old habits in a half way house for addicts called "The Giant Step," where one of our Touch Teams worked. When his wife finally withdrew from drugs, she had great physical pain; we helped her through an operation which she needed and stayed with her until she was on her feet. Her husband was afraid of her new faith-relationship—it threatened him. One Sunday when we were all in church, he literally grabbed her by her hair and took her back to the old life to shoot dope again. We could have broken his neck! It was a situation in which we had to learn to love this fellow for what he would one day become.

At this writing he has been withdrawn from heroin for the last five months. He works in a Christian coffee house. His changed life has helped his wife to return to a withdrawal, where Christ is Lord. How thankful we are that we did not say earlier, "Mister, if it weren't for you, maybe your wife wouldn't be back on heroin!" We learned to love him for what he could become, with Christ on the throne of his life!

5. *Recognize the Outsider's virtues.* One day, Jesus will use them.

He put them in the Outsider in the first place.

6. *Overlook his faults!* Only the Holy Spirit can change them any way, so why try to reform them?

7. *Be sensitive to the other's needs at all times.* Occasionally a Christian will forget about the Outsider's "frame of reference" and will assume needs to exist which do not exist at all. The Outsider may not *need* church, for example. What does he feel he needs? We must begin where *he* is, not where *we* are.

8. *Be a helping hand, but don't smother.* One Touch group learned a hard lesson about this principle when they lost an Outsider family's friendship because of "smother love." They wanted so desperately to relate that they seemed to be constantly "in the way." Feeling an invasion of their privacy, the family decided, "Whoa! This friendship is too much, too fast!"

9. *Allow time for the Holy Spirit to do His work.* I suppose all Christians tend to be impatient with Outsiders who dissipate precious years in self-life. Our deep burden for their salvation should keep us on our knees, rather than propel us into a premature confrontation. Trust in the work of the Holy Spirit! Don't try to do His work. In God's timetable, the salvation of the unbeliever will occur. Believe in Him!

10. *Be transparently OPEN—so that Christ can reveal Himself through* you. If your life is only partially yielded, you will not "be genuine" in every situation. How devastating to the Lord's work it is when a Christian "fakes" a personality. Be real! The only thing more disgusting than a preacher who uses a "holy voice" to deliver his sermon is a Christian who fakes a "holy life" in relating to an Outsider!

Classification of Pre-Evangelism

There are five basic areas where needs exist in the Outsider's life: *social, emotional, spiritual, intellectual, physical.* Relationships develop around these needs.

For example, a San Antonio couple, both college graduates with a major in drama, had a deep concern for their Outsider friends in the world of dramatics. They came to me, asking for help in

SOME CLASSIFICATIONS OF PRE-EVANGELISM

TOUCH POINTS

NEED	EXPOSURE	SKILLS
SOCIAL	RECREATION (Bridge, Golf, Fishing, Bowling, 42, etc.)	Limited to great ability
	SOCIAL GROUPS (Country Club, YMCA, Health Clubs, Civic Clubs, Sororities, Lodges, Bars & Private Clubs, Coffee Houses, etc.)	None. . .
EMOTIONAL	CARE GROUPS (Divorcees, Sick, Parents of problem children, Drug users, Alcoholics, People in crisis, Marital upheavals, etc.)	Training on a non-professional level
	CONCERN GROUPS (Meals sent in, help to newcomers in community, etc.)	None. . .
SPIRITUAL	FELLOWSHIP GROUPS (Weekday Bible Study, Prayer Cells, etc.)	Limited Training (Communication, Small groups)
	KID'S GROUPS ("Touch Time" Bible training groups, etc.)	
INTELLECTUAL	SHARE GROUPS (Internationals, Laubach Literacy classes, Atheists' Club, etc.)	Limited Training
PHYSICAL	ACTIVITY GROUPS (Ball teams, Exercise groups, etc.)	Knowledge of sports and health rules

THE POSSIBILITIES ARE ENDLESS!

Fig. 25

finding a way to TOUCH their friends. I first introduced them to a marvelous Christian actress in Houston, Jeannette Clift, who started the After Dinner Players as a ministry to Outsider young people interested in drama.

Jeannette has demonstrated Christ's compassion for Outsiders as much as any person I have known. She has written marvelous Bible-based plays, including *Ibid.* and *Op. Cit.,* which carried the redemptive message *to the players as well as the audience.* Through months of rehearsals and loving conversations, nearly all of the After Dinner Players came to accept Christ as Lord.

Following their visit with Jeannette, the couple got busy. The wife stayed up many nights until 4:00 A.M. writing a script based on Genesis which would make an impact upon the actors themselves. Their drama group consisted solely of unbelievers.

Christians make a tragic mistake by not infiltrating local secular clubs and organizations. They are perfect places *to meet Outsiders.* Those who object that this "takes time away from the Church" need to struggle with the fact that *the church takes God's people out of their mission field!*

"The People Who Care" in Houston have used the TOUCH symbol and the word *TOUCH* as the structure for many outreach ministries. They wear nylon jackets with the emblem imprinted, carry calling cards with the TOUCH emblem, and place stickers on cash registers in bars, restaurants, etc.

TOUCH

"The people who care" may be reached at any time of the day or night by calling

497 2420

Fig. 26

It is enough for Outsiders to know us *first* as "The People Who Care" from *TOUCH.* Eventually, they may learn about West Memorial—but by that time we are not considered "Baptists" who are trying to get a "notch on our gun."

Emotional needs are rampant in our society, and provide many opportunities for TOUCH ministries. Consider the divorced woman, for example.

In a TOUCH care group for divorcees, I learned from the women that most of them go through similar reaction stages following the breakup of their marriage: (1) *Anger* toward the husband, who often acts like a "rat" during legal proceedings; (2) *Loneliness* and *tears,* with Saturday being the worst day of the week; (3) *Fright,* when she realizes she doesn't know how to care for an automobile, repair a sticking door, etc.; (4) *Financial distress,* when the limited income really hits; (5) *Hate for "all men"*—for the only ones who now pay attention to her have sex-centered interests; (6) finally, the *snap-out-of-it* stage, when self-pity turns to awareness that she can't stop the world and get off.

How can divorcees find the genuine solutions to their heartaches until the *church* changes its pious and sticky self-righteous attitude? How dare we "sweep them under the rug"? Three out of ten adults and seven out of ten teen-agers who marry will get a divorce! TOUCH points are needed in *every community* to help these precious people find Christ during the most traumatic time of their lives.

What about the sick, the parents of problemed children, the drug users, the alcoholics, all the people in crisis? One woman in my church has contacts with those whose crisis is reported in the newspaper. When she reads about a family in trouble, her concern is "What is that poor wife going through?" Another person might say, "She probably has relatives! Why should I call on her at a time like that?"

Why? Because that wife has a hole in her heart! Betty, that dear Christian mother in my church, asked me to go with her to visit that wife she has read about. We drove across Houston to a small trailer house. The wife was awed by me—"a Preacher"—but poured her heart out to Betty in the privacy of the bedroom. That day, Betty won the woman to Christ. She had had no church contact at all!

We have discovered that a "must" requirement for Touch groups working in areas of emotional needs is a *basic training*. Dr. Juanita Hart, a psychiatrist in our congregation, is now writing a book specifically for this purpose, to be titled *Brick by Brick*. At the present time, we use Earl Jabay's *Search for Identity* (Zondervan), and *Your Inner Child of the Past,* by W. Hugh Missildine (Simon and Schuster). If a Christian has a basic understanding of the emotional needs of a human being, he can often help people who are not severely neurotic or psychotic—*just by loving and listening!*

Of course, it is important that Christians not get in over their heads with someone who is really emotionally sick; they should refer these to a pastor or physician. Many people, however, don't need a thing in the world except a *listening ear.* In a large California metropolis, there are ads in the personal columns of newspapers that read, "Lonely? Need someone to listen? Call (telephone number) 24 hours a day. Nontrained, unskilled listeners available, $35.00 an hour." In response to the calls, people with only a high school education will go to the caller's home and sympathetically listen. People are helped therapeutically by this. A TOUCH group could be formed just to care about people in crises. Through it many could be brought to know Jesus Christ as their Lord.

Concern groups may send meals to a family with Mother in the hospital, provide counsel to newcomers in the community, etc. Spiritual needs of Outsiders precipitate TOUCH weekday Bible studies, prayer cells, etc.

Children's TOUCH Time groups, using Child Evangelism Fellowship materials, have resulted in many, many Houston families being exposed to the gospel through converted children.

Intellectual opportunities to TOUCH unbelievers can include *Share groups.* For example, international women who are living in our area are learning English through the Laubach Literacy method, giving our women a one-to-one contact with Buddhists. Limited training of Christians is needed, and the possibilities are endless!

It is impossible to suggest the particular TOUCH ministries a group of Christians in a church should consider for their area. The *culture in the community* and the *Spirit-given direction to minister* are all-important factors.

In Pre-Evangelism, the Christian becomes a reflector of Christ, to be used by the Holy Spirit in the Outsider's life. John 3:3 reminds us, "Unless a man has been born over again he cannot *see* the kingdom of God." When the Outsider cannot *see* the kingdom, he must be exposed to its *reflection. You are a mirror!* You reflect Christ's reign in your life into the darkness of the Outsider's life. Through that reflection, the Holy Spirit expands the unbeliever's "field of consciousness," revealing sin and righteousness and judgment. Only the Holy Spirit can help the Outsider see his need:

A man in a windowless room cannot see the brightness of the sun.

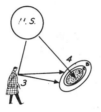

So with the windowless Outsider. Christ is reflected <u>into</u> his body and soul as the Holy Spirit opens mind, eyes, ears; the Spirit TOUCHes his spirit.

Fig. 27

How will the Outsider discover the love of God? We can reflect Jesus Christ to his natural eyes, and through his natural ears we can give him an awareness of the living Christ. We can share Christ through his *mind,* his *emotions,* and his *will.* The Holy Spirit, at the same time, ministers Christ *into his spirit,* for that is His task: When "your Advocate has come . . . he will bear witness to me. And you also are my witnesses, because you have been with me from the first." My Spirit-filled witness enters through his *body* and *soul;* the Spirit witnesses to his spirit in a manner beyond my understanding.

Use the following worksheet to prayerfully examine your area's needs. Where are you going to find *"holes in hearts?"*

WORKSHEET

This worksheet is designed to assist you in discovering the built-in areas of your life where you can be Christ's witness. Remember—the demonstration of a SPIRIT-FILLED LIFE is a CHRIST-SHARING LIFE!

I. CONSIDER YOUR NEIGHBORHOOD

1. List the families within 100 yards of your house or apartment, known by you to be unsaved: _____

_____

2. Who might be the *key person* in each home through which the gospel might be implanted? List their names:_____

_____

3. How could you most effectively develop pre-evangelism relationships with these families? _____

_____

II. CONSIDER TOUCH MINISTRIES

1. Review the classifications of pre-evangelism. To which areas of involvement with people are you most naturally fitted? social_____; emotional_____; spiritual_____; intellectual_____; physical_____.

2. What is the *Lord* calling you to do in terms of a TOUCH outreach ministry?_____

_____

Fig. 28

For example, down the block from you lives the Outsider Smith family. You may feel the key to reaching them will be the new friendship you have with their teen-age son, who has helped you build a shed. How could you most effectively develop that friendship with young Bill? He likes to fish! Perhaps you could take him and your own teen-aged son fishing. As you get to know him better, you will learn what his mother and father enjoy doing. You could then invite them over to dinner, inviting Bill too, and get to know them better. From that relationship, an expanding friendship can develop, through which they may discover Christ for themselves.

Which areas of involvement with people are you most naturally fitted for? Can you envision yourself working in an area of social needs, emotional needs, spiritual needs, intellectual or physical needs?

Most important, ask "What would my Lord have me to do in

terms of a *TOUCH Ministry?*" You are the means of sharing Christ with a particular world of people, the circle which is your private world. No one lives in it but you. No one can win it but you.

Isn't it time to get started?

NOTES

1. Haney, chapter 2.
2. George Morris, *Imperatives for Evangelism* (Nashville: General Board of Evangelism of The Methodist Church, 1967).

Chapter 8
Evangelism: Spirit-Filled
or Flesh-Centered?

Myron Augsburger defines evangelism as *"witness, with the intent of persuasion."* Delete "the intent of persuasion," and you do not have evangelism! However, *persuasion* does not mean *coercion,* nor does it merely refer to bringing the Outsider to an intellectual acceptance of Jesus Christ. Persuasion occurs when a genuinely Christ-filled life functions under Christ's reign in an unmistakable fashion, demonstrating the validity of the gospel. Evangelism is more than just doing something nice for someone who is sick, or providing a meal for one who is hungry. *Evangelism involves persuading people to receive Jesus Christ as Lord.*

Contrast two levels of evangelism, both used in today's churches: *Flesh-centered evangelism* is best defined as "all I can do, apart from Jesus Christ." This kind of evangelism is in wide use today. It promotes, publicizes, and in general functions on the level of a three-ring circus. It usually attracts people to Christ so that a secondary goal can be reached, such as building the biggest church in town.

Spirit-filled evangelism is defined as "all Christ does, apart from my efforts." In this kind of evangelism, the Christ who dwells in us reveals *Himself* to a lost world. It is the most significant evangelism in terms of building Christ's Kingdom. It has one desire: to *authentically* relate people to Jesus Christ, not only through an initial "profession of faith," but also through the nurture of the baby Christian to observe all He has commanded.

Flesh-centered evangelism is prevalent today; let us pray for it to die quickly, for it does more harm than good! Unfortunately, *flesh-centered evangelism produces flesh-centered converts.* What can be worse than a congregation of flesh-centered Christians working hard in the church organizations, trying to see how much they can accomplish by their own efforts?

Peter practiced *Spirit-filled evangelism.* As a result, God worked in unusual ways through him. In Acts 3:12 Peter said: "Men of Israel, why be surprised at this? Why stare at us as if we had made this man walk by some power or godliness of our own?" Peter knew Who was doing miracles! The results of his ministry came from the power of the Lord. Neither promotional schemes nor crowds attracted by a celebrity could possibly explain what happened as a result of his activity.

Flesh-centered evangelism, on the other hand, magnifies programs or exalts a church. Not long ago my secretary showed me a church bulletin. She had underlined this statement for me to read: "We are working our programs, and God is blessing our programs." In the margin she had written, "What a pity!" *God has not promised to bless "programs"! God blesses Spirit-filled lives!* Big churches can be made bigger with razzle-dazzle promotions, but the style of evangelism which will provide our next generation of Spirit-filled believers will be the kind in which the living Christ reveals Himself through the lives of yielded Christians.

Spirit-filled evangelism will magnify Jesus as Lord. It will be based on the conviction that it is enough to praise Him and to raise His banner: He *will* draw all men unto Himself if He is lifted up!

Spirit-filled evangelism may function in a large auditorium where

Christ is exalted, but it may also be found in a bar where a Christian sits drinking a coke, telling the man on the next stool about the Master. It may also be found operating in a home where a Christian has consistently revealed Christ's life to relatives who mock and scoff.

Flesh-centered evangelism occurs when carnal Christians do not share more than "how to be saved." As a result, their evangelism robs the convert of the full truth about salvation. Converts are not told that Christ offers freedom from the *penalty* of sin (a point-in-time occurrence) and also freedom from the *power* of sin (a day-by-day activity). Many times flesh-centered evangelism will not speak of anything but the penalty of sin. As with Jack Taylor, such victims of flesh-centered evangelism "sit down" to wait for heaven to come along, missing the growth which is the heritage of the Christian.

Spirit-filled evangelism requires Christians to be dethroned, Christowned, and Christ-operated. It emphasizes the importance of helping a baby Christian understand *more* than how to get an "Assurance Policy" so when he dies he won't "fry." It will explain the full truth of what it means to let Christ be Lord.

God is sick of *flesh-centered evangelism.* The world is waiting for the real expression of an authentic walk with Christ. That expression requires Spirit-directed men and women. G. D. Watson has said, "Make up your mind that God is an infinite Sovereign, and has a right to do as He pleases with His own . . . if you absolutely sell yourself to be His love slave, He will wrap you in a jealous love, and bestow upon you many blessings which come only to those who are in the inner circle."[1] Only those who are His "love slaves" will authentically bring this world to Christ!

Impact communion (see chap. 6) is the communication form for Spirit-filled evangelism. It is at this "brass tacks" communication level that Christ is shared with Mr. Outsider. With an Outsider not yet under conviction, *we witness.* With the Outsider who is under conviction, *we harvest.*[2] There is a distinct difference in the way we share Christ with one who is under conviction and one who is not.

A witness has been defined as "one who furnishes evidence." Again, the emphasis focuses upon the necessity for the Spirit-filled life. Our impact does not come only with what we *say* about Jesus, but by what we can demonstrate about His real presence in our own lives. Gabriel Marcel described it with these words: "I am obliged to bear witness because I hold, as it were, a particle of light; and to keep it to myself would be equivalent to extinguishing it."

The witness declares with his lips the truth about the One who sits on his life's throne, but he must also validate by his life what his lips reveal. The Holy Spirit then uses the verbal witness to TOUCH Outsiders and make them long for Christ's Lordship.

Spirit-filled evangelism involves:

1. Speaking
  2. To an Outsider
    3. From my personal experience
      4. With Jesus Christ, *my* Lord.

Remove any one of those factors, and something is lost. (1) Spirit-filled evangelism is more than silently living the Christian life: *it involves verbalizing the "good news."* (2) Spirit-filled evangelism does not occur unless I am sharing my life *with an Outsider.* (3) The Christ I share must be a *personal* Christ, not just Matthew's or Mark's or Luke's version. (4) Finally, evangelism is not just discussing one's membership in a church, but sharing Jesus Christ, *my* Lord.

In Chapter 5 of *Witness, Take the Stand!* I used this outline to help Christians think through the testimony of their conversion experience.[3] Thousands of Christians have discovered that these facts can be shared in less than two minutes—and many have come to receive Christ through the impact of these testimonies.

1. MY LIFE AND ATTITUDES BEFORE FOLLOWING
   CHRIST:

_____

_____

_____

_____

2. HOW I REALIZED MY PROBLEM:

_____

_____

_____

_____

3. HOW I BECAME A CHRISTIAN:

_____

_____

_____

_____

4. WHAT BEING A CHRISTIAN MEANS TO ME:

_____

_____

_____

_____

"Seed-sowing," or dropping your testimony into the lives of people you meet, can be an exciting part of the Spirit-filled walk. Areas of the everyday life where a _natural testimony_ can be shared include the service station, grocery store, bank lobby, restaurant, office, school, gymnasium, garden club, etc. Jesus suggested in Matthew 28:18-20 that _"as we go,"_ we are to make disciples. Only when the laity carry Christ squarely into the middle of our culture will His presence make _impact!_

If it is necessary for us to go back twenty years (or even) twenty months) or to our conversion experience to find the details of a vital relationship with Christ, we are in spiritual trouble. Often our most significant testimony may center around _recent_ events of our life in which Christ has "taken over," Perhaps you have never reflected upon the details of your spiritual pilgrimage and are unaware of the many rich experiences you have had through Christ. Included in them may well be the details of how your carnal life was moved to yield to Christ's Lordship, to be controlled by His Holy Spirit.

The first graph is a sample of a completed "pilgrimage." It will demonstrate what one person's pilgrimage included. As you scan it, consider your own spiritual history. Then, using the blank graph which follows, chart your own pilgrimage. There are 22 vertical lines; divide them into the length of time you have been a Christian, numbering them by months or years. Using "O" as *average,* use the scale on the *right* to express sorrows or tragedies you have experienced. Determine the intensity by the number selected; *i.e.,* "7" would be despair close to suicide. Use the scale on the *left*

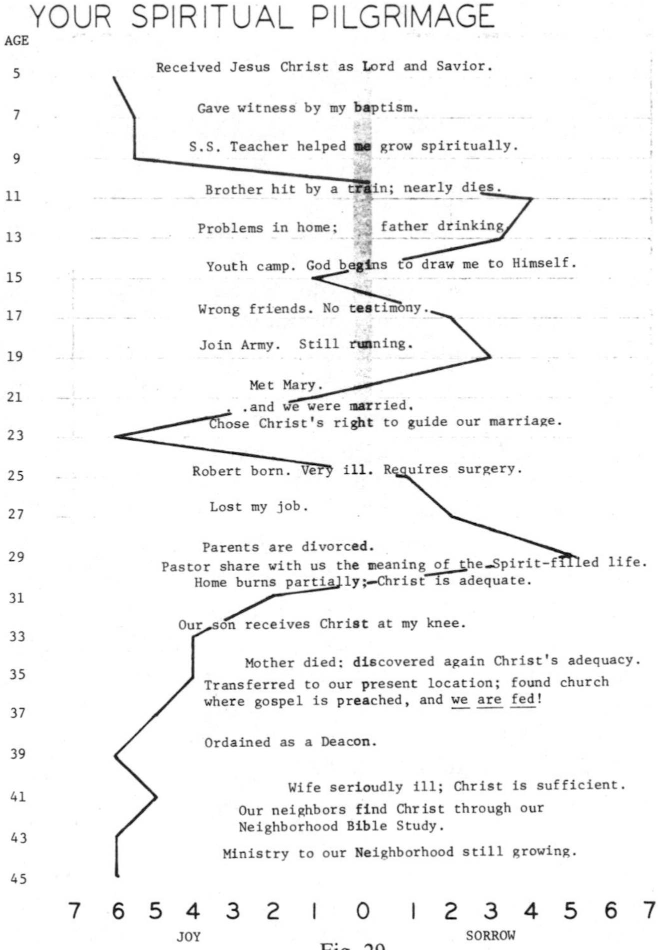

YOUR SPIRITUAL PILGRIMAGE

AGE

5 — Received Jesus Christ as Lord and Savior.

7 — Gave witness by my baptism.

9 — S.S. Teacher helped me grow spiritually.

11 — Brother hit by a train; nearly dies.

13 — Problems in home; father drinking.

15 — Youth camp. God begins to draw me to Himself.

17 — Wrong friends. No testimony.

19 — Join Army. Still running.

21 — Met Mary.
    .and we were married.
    Chose Christ's right to guide our marriage.

23

25 — Robert born. Very ill. Requires surgery.

27 — Lost my job.

29 — Parents are divorced.
    Pastor share with us the meaning of the Spirit-filled life.
    Home burns partially; Christ is adequate.

31

33 — Our son receives Christ at my knee.

35 — Mother died; discovered again Christ's adequacy.
    Transferred to our present location; found church
    where gospel is preached, and we are fed!

37

39 — Ordained as a Deacon.

41 — Wife serioudly ill; Christ is sufficient.
    Our neighbors find Christ through our
    Neighborhood Bible Study.

43 — Ministry to our Neighborhood still growing.

45

7 6 5 4 3 2 1 0 1 2 3 4 5 6 7
JOY   SORROW

Fig. 29

to express your periods of joy, cleansing, and victory. Here the number "7" would characterize the highest level of joy you can experience. By "reliving" the past years of your Christian life, you will be made aware of the hand of God patiently forming the image of Christ in you. Sharing these details with others will be a blessing as you recall what God has done for you.

YOUR SPIRITUAL PILGRIMAGE

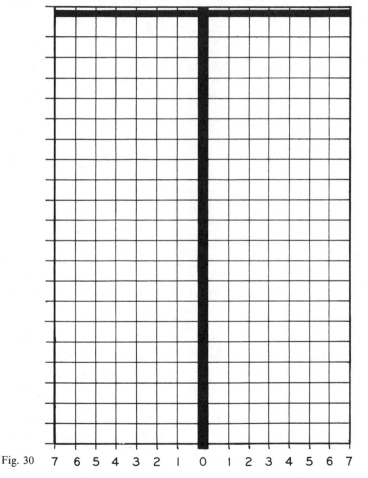

Fig. 30   7   6   5   4   3   2   1   0   1   2   3   4   5   6   7

Completing this chart has been a tremendous blessing to many Christians. When I have asked groups to share these experiences fo God's grace, we have often finished with nearly everyone near tears and with prayers of thanksgiving for what God has done.

Spirit-filled evangelism may not only use the *written* record of God's activity in the lives of men, but may also use the *living* record of Christ's work in today's generation of Christians. This powerful statement of His moving within our own lives can guide scoffing Outsiders to see that they are empty sieves until they, too, experience the Lordship of Jesus Christ for themselves!

AS THE CHRISTIAN SERVES...

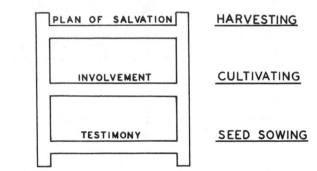

PLAN OF SALVATION	HARVESTING
INVOLVEMENT	CULTIVATING
TESTIMONY	SEED SOWING

Fig. 31

THE TWO LADDERS OF EVANGELISM

The two ladders of evangelism in the following illustrations help to demonstrate the various levels at which Christ is shared:

The first ladder shows the steps by which the Christian shares his Lord. The first responsibility we have is to *sow seed*. That is, we share our testimony. It may include our conversion experience or something that happened just this morning. By a handful of words, we leave friends or strangers with an *awareness that God is in this world, working in human lives.*

The second rung on the ladder is *cultivating*. This ministry is performed with those whom God has made "significant others" in our lives. This level of evangelism includes not only a verbal testimony, but also *involvement* with these persons. Some of that involvement may not "preach," yet may be more powerful than any sermon in demonstrating Christ's love and forgiveness.

The third rung on the ladder is *harvesting.* The source for all we do here is the *written Word of God.* Scripture is used to explain how one becomes a Christian. Before it is time to explain salvation's plan, there must be *the convicting presence of the Holy Spirit within the life of the Outsider.* After He has spoken, then we speak, sharing the simple steps by which the Second Birth takes place.

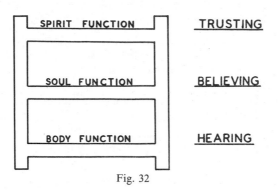

Fig. 32

The second ladder explains how the Outsider responds to Christ's call. Dr. Oswald J. Smith has preached a sermon which is the inspiration for Figure 32. He describes three steps by which Outsiders come to receive the Lord Jesus and become children of God.

The first step is *hearing.* Because a man lives in America, it does not necessarily mean he has "heard" the gospel all his life. Sometime ago I visited in the home of a man in his thirties. I said, "Has anyone ever explained to you how one goes about becoming a Christian?"

He said, "No, Ralph, this has never been explained to me."

I replied, "I'm so sorry that you live in a Christian America and no person has ever shared this truth with you. May I do so now?"

He gladly gave me permission, and in the next few minutes I shared salvation truth with him.

As I left his house with the pastor of that family, he said to me, "Ralph, I sat in the same chair you just used in his living room, and just one month ago I shared those same Scriptures verses with that man! Why did he tell you he 'had never heard'?"

I smiled and said, "What does the Scripture say about that?"

He then replied with a knowing look, "Having ears to hear, they will not hear!"

He was exactly right! Just because a man has attended Sunday School and church all his life does *not* mean he has *heard* a thing! We need to communicate on a personal, eyeball-to-eyeball level with Outsiders before we will be able to discover whether they have ever really *heard* the gospel.

Perhaps you have had the experience of purchasing a new automobile. For the first time in your life you begin to "see" all of the automobiles on the road made by the same manufacturer. Why? You have a *new awareness* of that model of car. Outsiders experience a similar pattern in their spiritual awareness. Through relating to a Christian, they are "sensitized" to Christ's presence. For the first time in years, they may begin to "hear" the gospel message. Although that message has been shared all along, the Holy Spirit is only now beginning to develop their awareness of these truths.

The next rung on the ladder is *believing*. As Dr. Smith points out, the Kings James translators mistranslated the Greek word for "trust" (*pisteus*) in the New Testament. In the King James translation of the Old Testament, wherever that same Greek word occurred in the Septuagint, it was translated "trust," but in the New Testament, for some unexplainable reason, the translators changed that word to "believe." For example, John 3:16 should read, "For God *trusteth* in him should not perish, but have everlasting life." Where the King James reads, "*Believe* on the Lord Jesus Christ and thou shalt be saved," the Greek word for "believe" should be translated "trust." How many church members there must be who have "believed" in Jesus, when in reality they have never taken the step of *trust*, which alone brings eternal life!

What is "believing"? It always follows hearing—but does not always follow! Just because we *hear* something does not mean we *believe* it.

Two years ago in the Orient, I told a simple peasant that a man from the United States had walked on the moon. *He heard it, but he did not believe it!* It was too fantastic a piece of knowledge for a near-primitive man to *believe*.

I might assure you that a red chair near me as I write this is a good, solid chair and that it would hold your weight if you sat in it. You have *heard* about the chair. You will probably be willing to climb to the second rung on our ladder and *believe* my statement to be true: you accept the fact that my chair would support your weight. However, you are sitting in another chair as you read this. My red chair is empty! You have not *trusted* the red chair. If you were to *trust* it, you would come to my room and actually sit in it.

How many people there must be who have *believed* in Jesus Christ without having *trusted* Him with their lives! Trust involves surrendering one's life to the Lordship of Jesus Christ. When we share salvation truths with Outsiders, we must be sure they do not stop short of trusting.

Recently I went to visit a young woman who had publicly "accepted Christ" and wanted to join the church. I said, "Tell me what has happened in your life."

She replied, "Well, I went forward in the church."

I said, "Why did you go forward?"

She answered, "Because I was ready to believe in Jesus."

I said, "Tell me what believing in Jesus means to you."

She said, "Well, you know: you believe in God, you believe in heaven, you believe in the Bible, and you believe in Jesus."

I asked, "Do you know what I mean when I use the phrase "trusting Jesus"?

She said, "I'm not sure."

I explained that it is not enough just to believe with the mind that Jesus existed. I explained that we must go one step beyond such belief, *turning our life over to Him* so that He is trusted to be the Master of all we are.

I said, "For you to become a Christian means you will relinquish any further rights to live a life that is not according to God's will. From now on, God's will shall become your will. Have you yet *trusted* your life to Christ's direction, saying, "Jesus, I trust you to live in my life, think my thoughts, walk my walk, and guide me in the days ahead. When I get ready to marry, I will find your husband; when I get ready to go to college, I will find your college? Is this what you were saying when you came forward last Sunday?"

She said stiffly, "No, that's not what I did last Sunday, and I am not about to do that!"

I said, "Why don't we just continue to think and pray about this for awhile? Perhaps it is too soon for you to consider church membership and baptism. Shall we wait until you are ready to *trust* Him?"

If we had not talked about the difference between *believing* and *trusting,* that young lady would have joined the church! In later years she might transfer her letter eight or nine times, always being "accepted" as a Christian—and I earnestly believe she would have gone straight to hell when she died! *Spirit-filled evangelism will bring a person to the point where he or she is aware of a constant, continuing surrender to Christ's Lordship.*

Some years ago I shared Christ's love with a man who attended church week after week with his dear Christian wife. I said to him, "You are a wonderful father to your sons. You attend church. We play golf together, and I know you like me as your friend. Yet I know you are not a Christian. What is holding you back?"

He said, "Ralph, I have been listening to you for months, and I confess I have problems believing in some of the miracles in the Bible. This matter of the Virgin Birth has always bothered me, for example. I have an idea, however, that all those doubts might fade overnight if I could get one big problem settled."

I said, "What is that?"

He looked me in the eye and said, "I am not anywhere near

ready to give my life away, to permit it to be controlled by anyone else—not even God!"

I might have preached an easier "believism" message, and he might have joined my church. Instead, we was wrestling with the relationship of *trust*. I said, "You are so honest! Refusal to come under Christ's control is the primary act of rebellion for each one of us; we must face it squarely before Christ can enter our lives."

He agonized over the matter! He sat in the pew week after week, struggling with trust. I would drink coffee with him in his home, and we would struggle with his personal rebellion. Only after several months of fighting God's claim of total ownership did he *trust* Christ. Ever since, his life has been filled with growth and commitment. He was worth praying for!

When all pastors begin to clearly preach the biblical truth that salvation begins with trust, our "statistics" may drop off for a period—*but the Lamb's Book of Life will begin to grow!*

Notes

1. G. D. Watson "Others May, You Cannot" (Westchester, Ill.: Good News Publishers).

2. This is developed at greater length in *Witness, Take the Stand!* available from Evangelism Division, Baptist General Convention of Texas, 306 Baptist Building, Dallas, Texas 75201.

3. Neighbour, pp. 36-37.

Chapter 9
Getting the Lost Saved and the Saved Filled

Miss Bertha Smith told me one day, "Our greatest sin in caring for baby Christians is not teaching them how to live triumphantly. It is, however, the *second* greatest sin of flesh-centered evangelism.

There is an even greater sin connected with this evangelism. I would like to add to hers, *the sin of delivering still-born "baby Christians" who are dead from "birth"!*

THE FIRST SIN: STILL-BORN CHRISTIANS

It is possible for a person to be led through the mechanics of accepting Christ, followed by baptism, church membership, and active service, *without genuine conversion!* "Soulish" conversion involves only the activity of mind, emotion, and will—*not the spirit.* The person has soul-motivating *belief,* but not a Christ-filled *life.* Flesh-centered evangelism has undoubtedly produced thousands of "Christians" like this. A valid Lordship has not been initiated, and there is no witness of the Spirit (1 John 4:13).

Consider Figure 33.

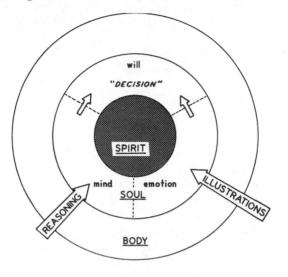

Fig. 33

Let me illustrate. Manley Beasley tells of a profession of faith made by a young woman who possessed questionable morals. Elated, he told her father of his delight over her decision. The father said slowly, "Manley, I am glad she made this profession of her faith. I trust she meant it. I have seen her 'commit herself to Christ' many times before; what I am waiting for is the time when I see evidence that *God has committed Himself to her.* What He starts, He finishes!"

Any act of *genuine commitment* by a person will be authenticated by God's obvious activity within that life. If the Spirit of God genuinely enters the spirit of man, His divine activity will be experienced by the convert. The result of authentic commitment will always be God's continuous shaping us to the likeness of His Son. Those whom He justifies, He also gives His splendour (Romans 8:29-30). It is obvious from many scriptures that God's purpose for man is precisely this: *His life is now mine, molding me to be conformed to Christ's likeness.*[1] He does not wait for any charismatic "experience" to initiate His divine work of pottery molding—it is initiated *from the second of conversion* and is the *proof* of genuine salvation.

Salvation does not necessarily begin when someone "walks the aisle," but it always begins with a motion of the *heart* in which God initiates His residence within the life. The degree of faith this requires need be no deeper than that which it takes for God to commit Himself to live within us. The great principle underlying Old Testament sacrifices was that *God must accept sacrifice.* He knows our innermost heart and is aware of the soulish reasons which motivate "decisions." The repentant heart is never spurned by Him; the unrepentant one, regardless of many tears or tithes, is never accepted.

Flesh-centered evangelists today often berate and ridicule the "liberals" who have taken away the deity of Christ, while they are often signally guilty of the opposite heresy: *humanizing the way the sinner comes to Christ.*

It is pure humanism to so elevate the importance of the sinner's "decision to receive Christ" that conversion is directed toward the human will, mind, and emotions. The human decision is *not* the critical factor in salvation, nor is "faith" something a man turns on as though it were a light switch. Conversion is an act of grace—initiated, produced, and completed by God.

Speaking of such humanistic theology, Charles Haddon Spurgeon wrote that what some evangelists were trying to do was "arouse man's activity; what we want to do is kill it once and for all, to show him that he is lost and ruined, and that his activities are not now at all equal to the work of conversion; that he must look upward. *They* seek to make the man stand up; *we* seek to bring him down, and make him feel that there he lies in the hand of God, and that his business is to submit himself to God, and cry aloud, 'Lord, save, or we perish.' We hold that man is never so near grace as when he begins to feel he can do nothing at all. When he says, 'I can pray, I can believe, I can do this, and I can do the other,' marks of self-sufficiency and arrogance are on his brow." [2]

The very act of trusting Christ is the result of the work of the

Holy Spirit within a man. This cannot be initiated simply because the Annual Revival Meeting has arrived. The whole plan of redemption is God-initiated. To forget this truth is to present a salvation appeal for man's mind, emotion, and will to "receive Christ." The response to the appeal will be (apart from God's grace) a still-born "Christian." Let it be remembered that the conversion of a soul is a *creation*. A child never "chooses" the moment he comes from the womb; the second birth offers the sinner no more choice than the first. The term "regeneration" refers to the instant *act* of God in implanting new life in a person.

The fact that God initiates regeneration should be enough to terminate all invitation to "be born again, if you are ready." Our task as Christians is to declare to Outsiders "that they must be saved by grace through faith, and that trust in Christ is the way to peace with God." [3]

Perhaps the most profound expression of counseling the unconverted in how to seek Christ is found in Spurgeon's preaching.

> Before you leave this place, . . . breathe an earnest prayer to God, saying, "God be merciful to me a sinner. Lord, I need to be saved. Save me. I call upon thy name." Join with me in prayer at this moment, I entreat you. Join with me while I put words in your mouths, and speak them on your behalf—"Lord, I am guilty, I deserve thy wrath. Lord, I cannot save myself. Lord, I would have a new heart and a right spirit, but what can I do? Lord, I can do nothing, come and work in me to will and to do of they good pleasure.
>
> > Thou alone hast power, I know
> > To save a wretch like me;
> > To whom, or whither should I go
> > If I should run from thee?
>
> But I now do from my very life call upon thy name. Trembling, yet believing, I cast myself wholly upon thee, O Lord. I trust the blood and righteousness of thy dear Son . . . Lord, save me tonight, for Jesus' sake." [4]

In Figure 34, an authentic conversion is seen to be the result of the power of God. The life has received the Lord Jesus Christ, and prompt evidence of His presence will confirm the convert's regeneration.

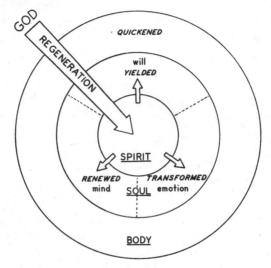

Fig. 34

Those ministering to Outsiders will receive the witness of the Spirit when the harvest is ready for *reaping*. Let there be a holy shrinking away from *stealing unripened grain*.

While this final chapter is written to suggest the nature of the counseling *message* (methods are legion!) for Outsiders, perhaps it should first be shared with the *members* of the congregation. Sadly, many of them will be "Outsiders" to these truths.

A recent survey of Southern Baptist pastors indicated they felt 50% of their church members had never experienced the new birth. If so, then it is a cardinal sin for these people to be allowed to swap church memberships and never be ministered to at the most basic level! Each one should be given opportunity to share an account of his or her spiritual pilgrimage with a counsellor.

At West Memorial Baptist Church, we have discovered that a *minimum* of four hours of counseling is necessary with the average Outsider before he is converted. (This does not include time spent in "pre-evangelism.") Children are given even more time and are not baptized until they reach an intellectual age when they can grasp the symbolical meaning of the act.

SUGGESTIONS FOR THE HARVESTER OF OUTSIDERS

1. *Be sure the seeker is under conviction.* The pastor of a large church said, "Will all pastors and mature Christians assist me in counseling those who have come forward to accept Christ?" I moved quickly from my seat and met a ten-year-old boy who had come forward.

My first question was, "Why did you come forward?"

His totally honest answer was, "Because my sister told me to."

He had absolutely no conviction placed in his heart by the Holy Spirit. Yet that day, in spite of my comments on the decision card that he had "come forward to confess his faith and *did not have the slightest idea what he was doing,*" I watched that pastor ready him for baptism! While that kind of "evangelism" makes baptismal headlines in state religious papers, a better name for it might be *spiritual rape.*

Let's not pick on the children, though. What about the man who joins the church because it's good for his insurance business or to keep his wife off his back? What about the couple who honestly told me they had joined the church to keep the church visitors off their back? Or the man who came from a church of another denomination "for the sake of religious harmony in our marriage." Until the Holy Spirit has brought Outsiders under conviction, they cannot—and should not—be brought to make a confession of faith in Christ, let alone baptism into the fellowship!

How is this to be measured? By the amount of tears shed? Not necessarily: a "death-bed illustration" at the end of the sermon might better account for the much weeping at the altar. *Conviction is the result of the Holy Spirit at work within the life.* He brings the awareness of (1) what I am—a sinner; (2) what God is—righteous; and (3) how uncrossable the gulf is—judgment. Conviction, or "cross-examination," is a condition of God-given sorrow over personal rebellion to His Lordship. It has little or nothing to do with the emotions, which only secondarily react to the spirit upheaval involved. Conviction is, above all else, *awareness:* the "field of consciousness" has opened wide to *Spirit-given facts.*

If conviction does not exist, the only honest thing to do for the person is to encourage the delay of any further public act. The counselor may permit this initial contact to develop into a regular time for fellowship and Bible study. *Salvation never occurs until preceded by conviction!*

2. *Be sure the seeker understands the meaning of SIN.* This *knowledge-level* truth must then pass from belief to trust. Unfortunately, 99% of Outsiders view "sin" as *action* rather than *condition.* To understand that "sin" is a *root* word and "sins" a *fruit* word will bring the unbeliever to an awareness that the basic problem in his life is not the cobweb, but the *spider.*

In scores of conversations between "soul winners" [5] and Outsiders, this matter is never clarified. While one discusses "sin," the other discusses "sins." First John 1:9 is written about "sins"—*to the Christian.* Romans 3:23 discusses "sin"—*with the Outsider.* His *condition* must be dealt with *at* the cross before his *actions* can be dealt with *by* the cross.

3. *Be sure the seeker is not taking out a "Life Assurance Policy."* Conversion must be equally focused upon the after-life and *this present life.* It shoud not relate primarily to the problem of going to heaven instead of hell, but to the Lordship of Jesus Christ in each hour of each day . . . from here through eternity!

To illustrate this, let me share the details of my brother David's tragic childhood accident. As a nine-year-old, he rode his bicycle into the side of a freight train engine. Caught in the long steel bar which connected the driver wheels, he was finally dropped along the tracks a hundred feet from the crossing. A fence which separated the eastbound tracks from the westbound tracks caused David's body to fall within inches of the speeding wheels. In semiconsciousness, he began to roll beneath them.

A hunchback named Cisco ran down the narrow passageway between fence and cars. Throwing himself between David and the rushing train, he held onto the fence for two dear lives.

That day Cisco became David's *savior.* A year later my brother still walked on crutches, but he was alive! In the years which have passed, however, David never felt a need to acknowledge Cisco's saving act as important enough for him to be both *savior and lord* of his life. David controlled his life without further advice from Cisco.

This can happen in a train accident—but never at Calvary! Salvation is always, always, ALWAYS a matter of here-and-now submission to Christ's continual control.

4. *Be sure the seeker's repentance is genuine.* Superficiality in the area of repentance will inevitably result in shallow obedience to His commands. Change of heart concerning the matter of-government is the very core and essence of salvation. It should be noted that a great danger here is the substitution of *self-deter-mined resolutions* for *Spirit-given repentance.* Repentance is not as much a matter of choosing God's rule as it is observing *the evidence that He has come to rule!* At conversion, the Outsider will manifest a God-given revulsion over past sin.

THE SECOND SIN: UNTAUGHT BABY CHRISTIANS

Our generation of clergymen ought to be pondering the large body of "carnal Christians" we have produced—while wearing sackcloth and ashes! It is questionable that all or even a large percentage of our "carnal brothers" are wheat; many tares are sown within the church. However, every pastor knows that a certain percentage of those he shepherds are like the little girl who fell out of bed, explaining, "I guess I fell asleep too close to where I crawled in."

Processes have been omitted which would have gone far toward altering the condition of young believers in our churches. They are thrust into ongoing merry-go round programs which do not even slow down long enough for them to climb aboard. "New member orientation programs" are just as unsatisfactory, usually dealing with "assurance, stewardship, church membership, and how the denomination functions."

Here are some principles of spiritual growth:

PRINCIPLE #1: GROWTH IN THE NEW CHRISTIAN REQUIRES ATTEN-
TION AND TIME.

Growth occurs at various rates in both physical and spiritual life. Realizing this, every sermon and many Bible lessons delivered at West Memorial Baptist Church are taped for sale through the TOUCH Tape Library of our fellowship. Almost daily these old messages are helpful to new people. My dear flock is scattered all along the pilgrimage pathway—from fighting alcohol's physical lust to struggling with the spiritual principle of reckoning in Romans 6:11. A sermon preached may be "right" for only 15 percent of the audience on the Sunday it is delivered; over several years, hundreds will be "ready" for it.

We also have a book table, offering books at every level for Christian growth. A book purchased two years ago by one woman is just now being "discovered" by her husband, who called me recently to discuss it.

The baby Christian should be cared for by a mature believer who will remain available for personal dialogue and nurture—indefinitely! When this is done, great profit will result from the relationship. Of course, we never lead another higher than we ourselves have been brought.

Miles J. Stanford has devoted his lifetime to the individual nurture of believers at various levels. His books are not written for clandestine distribution; rather, each one has been produced to be shared with a Christian "when ready" for growth truths.[6] He has taught me an all-important lesson regarding feeding lambs *when they are hungry.*

Further, it must be understood that growth takes time. Stanford writes:

> We might consider some familiar names of believers whom God obviously brought to maturity and used for His glory—such as Pierson, Chapman, Tauler, Moody, Goforth, Mueller, Taylor, Watt,

Trumbull, Meyer, Murray, Havergal, Guyon, Mabie, Gordon, Hyde, Mantle, McCheyne, McConkey, Deck, Paxson, Stoney, Saphir, Carmichael, and Hopkins. The *average* for these was fifteen years *after* they entered their life work before they began to know the Lord Jesus as their Life, and ceased trying to work for Him and began allowing Him to be their All in all and do His work through them. This is not to discourage us in any way, but to help us to settle down with our sights on eternity, by faith "apprehending that for which also we are apprehended to Christ Jesus, pressing toward the mark for the prize of the high calling of God in Christ Jesus" (Philippians 3:12b, 13).

Certainly this is not to discount a Spirit-fostered experience, blessing, or even a crisis; but it is to be remembered that these simply contribute to the over-all, the all-important PROCESS. It takes time to get to know ourselves; it takes time and eternity to get to know our Infinite Lord Jesus Christ. Today is the day to put our hand to the plow, and irrevocably set our heart on His goal for us—"that we may know Him; and the power of His ressurection, and the fellowship of His sufferings, being made conformable unto His death" (Philippians 3:10).[7]

If the new convert is properly nurtured, he need not experience the tragic vacuum-life described in Jack Taylor's *The Key to Triumphant Living.*[8] Nor will he necessarily need to duplicate the cataclysmic manner of being filled with the Holy Spirit that Taylor experienced. Even more precious will be his own Christian experience: he has been *baptized and filled with the Holy Spirit at the moment of conversion.* By daily acknowledging the inner work of the Within One and accepting days of sunshine or storm as a part of the growth process, the convert can experience the continual infilling of the Holy Spirit.

Is this not God's *perfect* way for the believer? God is anxious for each one of His children to know continuous growth throughout their lives. Perhaps each pastor today ought to divide his ministry into two facets: (1.) to provide adequate nurture to the new convert so that he will not follow in the steps of the Instant Carnal Christian; (2.) to enable the older carnal members to know and experience Christ as their Lord and their Life.

T. Austin-Sparks describes the ebb and flow of the normal growth tides in his book, *What Is Man?*

> There are stages in spiritual experience, more or less pronounced in different cases for certain reasons. The first phase may be a great and overflowing joy, with a marvelous sense of emancipation. In this phase extravagant things are often said as to total deliverance and final victory . . . then there may, and often does, come a phase of which inward conflict is the chief feature. It may be very much of a Romans vii experience. This will lead under the Lord's hand to several things; firstly, to the fuller knowledge of the meaning of identification with Christ, as in Romans vi. Happy the man who has been instructed in this from the beginning.[9]

As the work of God continues, "There may be crises in this course marked by definite and tremendous experiences. But no such crisis is final: every one has to have an outgrowth leading to greater fullnesses. It is fatal to relate everything to a crisis or experience of years ago, and to stop there."[10]

PRINCIPLE #2: GROWTH IN THE NEW CHRISTIAN WILL REQUIRE PROPER DOCTRINE.

The Outsiders who come to Christ are excited persons. Since they have not known a "cultural faith," there is a sharp contrast between their thirst for Scripture truth and that of their fossilized brothers who have dozed through years of sermons. These new converts must be carefully fed, for they are all the world like trusting baby birds with their beaks wide open, ready to swallow everything dropped into their mouths.

Without proper indoctrination, their enthusiasm "for all God has for me" can lead them to the pit of "holiness" error. Once they fall into that, years may elapse before the scars begin to fade.

First of all, the matter of the *baptism of the Holy Spirit* should be properly taught. The Scripture is clear: we are baptized by the Holy Spirit at conversion.[11] It is simply impossible to be born again without having received the Holy Spirit as the *seal* of our salvation, the *earnest* of our inheritance. "Tarrying at an altar for The Baptism" is false doctrine.

Secondly, *the filling of the Holy Spirit* should be understood.

It is *not* a single "experience." Ephesians 5:18 literally exhorts us, *"be being filled* with the Holy Spirit." The new believer's vital union from birth with the Holy Spirit includes *both His baptism and His filling.* Converts must understand that they have started their new life *filled*; it is not a new event to be sought, but a relationship to be continued—and continue it will, as long as we neither resist, lie to, grieve nor quench His work within us! A continual "agreeing with God" concerning sins will bring continual cleansing and the continual filling of the Spirit.

Thirdly, the *"Identification with Christ"* truths should be shared. The "Insider's" pilgrimage is possible because the Within One is now resident, come to shape him into the likeness of His Son. A full prayer life should be encouraged. Romans 6 through 8 may take years to fully comprehend, but a careful study of these chapters will provide a solid foundation for growth.

Emphasis should focus upon *what Christ will do* in the life, rather than morbid introspection about what *ought to be changed.* One has said, "If we can say 'in me dwelleth no good thing,' we have thought quite long enough about ourselves; let us then think about Him who thought about us with thoughts of good and not of evil, long before we had thought of ourselves at all. Let us see what His thoughts of grace about us are, and take up the words of faith, 'If God be for us, who can be against us?' "

PRINCIPLE #3: THE NEW CHRISTIAN SHOULD COMPREHEND HIS
SOURCE FOR WITNESS

It is Christ within! While scripture study and memorization may later bring clarity to the verbal witness, *the indwelling Spirit begins to witness at once through the new Christian.* The Spirit-filled convert usually discovers the "well of living water" flowing within him to the Outsiders in his world from the moment of conversion . . . and will be bewildered to observe many carnal "pillars" in the church who are as dry as the desert! He may have his disillusionment over this turned into a valuable lesson by his spiritual counselor. That is, *Christ-controlled lives are always compassion-filled lives.* It is an utter impossibility for one to be fully filled without freely flowing. Spirit-filled evangelism is simple. The One Who is not willing for any to perish will use us to accomplish His plans. He needs no help: if we will be nothing, He will be everything!

NOTES

1. For example, Philippians 1:6; Hebrews 9:14; 10:10,14; 1 John 3:2-11,24.
2. Ian H. Murray, *The Forgotten Spurgeon* (London: The Banner of Truth Trust, 1966), pp. 87-88.
3. Murray, p. 106.
4. Murray, pp. 107-108.
5. Can we not abolish this term as applied to humans? There is only *one* "soul winner" in the universe: the Holy Spirit! Further, He does not win a *soul* until he abides forever in a man's *spirit.*
6. Available from Christian Correspondence, Box 7507, Colorado Springs, Colorado 80907.
7. Miles J. Stanford, *The Green Letters* (Available from Christian Correspondence), pp. 8-9
8. Taylor, chapter 1.
9. T. Austin-Sparks, *What Is Man?* (Indianapolis: Premium Literature Company, n.d.), pp. 61-62.
10. Austin-Sparks, p. 62.
11. Acts 2:38, Ephesians 4:30; 1:14; 2 Corinthians 1:22; 5:5; John 15:26 with 1 John 5:7-10.

Epilogue

Dear reader, my book has come to the beginning end. It has not been written with the hope that it might be *read*, but *lived*! Last night I clipped a report from my newspaper, reporting that churchgoing in the United States in 1971 continued a thirteen-year downtrend. Since 1955, the percentage of adults of all faiths attending their place of worship in a typical week *has decreased from 49 percent to 40 percent.* The further breakdown reports only a 28 percent attendance among those aged twenty-one to twenty-nine years of age, with 37 percent of all Protestants and 19 percent of all Jews darkening church doors.

The TOUCH of the Spirit has been too long delayed! Moreover, before the TOUCH can begin, carnality among the members of God's family must stop. This problem alone, apart from Spirit-led repentance, may cause additional years of delay while our nation falls into an even deeper secularism. You who pass by, *does it bother you at all that the church today limits its ministry to less than forty out of one hundred Americans?*

This generation of Christians may just possibly be more like the Hebrews who were turned away from the promised land at Kadesh Barnea than any generation in modern times. Can God possibly fill us to TOUCH His world, or must we simply die off to make room for another generation that will not be enamored of buildings, programs, and cheap-grace-baptismal reports?

The new day calls for new men who have learned a new way to speak. Austin-Sparks has written, "If all the religious speech and preaching and talking about the gospel which goes on in one week were the utterance of the Holy Spirit, what a tremendous impact of God upon the world would be registered! But it is obviously not so and this impact is not felt." [1]

TOUCHing Outsiders is a ministry belonging only to those who are *born of the Spirit*, who have learned to speak His words, look through His eyes, love with His heart, touch with His hands, walk with His feet. Because we starve spiritually, the Outsiders perish!

I was called by God to be a missionary. My wife, Ruth, and I tried to go to Africa, but He stopped us. It took us years to recognize our mission field: Mr. and Mrs. Outsider! To you within the stained glass walls, I bring a call from those who die at your doorstep without Christ: come over and help us! Let the choir sing off key; let the valentine party be ill-planned; let the dear deacons miss a meeting—*but do not let the Outsiders around you die unTOUCHed on your doorstep!*

Stop! Wait! Don't rush to leave your lovely building yet: pause to pray and reflect awhile. That dear Outsider may be *lost*, but he is not *stupid. Are you real? Who do you reveal? Are you filled?*

Sir, they would see Jesus!

NOTES

1. Austin-Sparks, p. 80.

APPENDIX
Church Covenant
West Memorial Baptist Church
Houston, Texas

In the spirit of love, we have banded together to comprise a local expression of an *ecclesia,* which is the body of those on whom the call of God rests to witness to the grace and truth of God.

Because we believe that Jesus is the Christ, the Son of the Living God, we will seek to bring every phase of our lives under His Lordship.

We unreservedly and with abandon commit our lives and destiny to Christ, promising to give Him priority in all the affairs of life. We will seek first the Kingdom of God and His Righteousness.

We believe that God is the total owner of our lives and resources. We give God the throne in relation to the material aspects of our lives. Because God is a lavish giver, we too shall be lavish and cheerful in our regular gifts.

We commit ourselves, regardless to the expenditure of time, energy, and money to become informed, mature Christians.

We will seek to be Christ-led in all relations with our fellowmen, with other nations, groups, classes, and races.

We commit ourselves to watch over one another in brotherly love; to pray for each other; to aid one another in sickness and distress.

We recognize that the function of this *ecclesia* is to glorify God in adoration and sacrificial service, and to be God's missionaries in the world, bearing witness to God's redeeming grace in Jesus Christ.

Resources

I. The Spirit-Filled Life; Spirit-Filled Evangelism

Austin-Sparks, T.: *What Is Man?* (Indianapolis: Premium Literature Company, n.d.). Excellent expanded discussion about body, soul, and spirit.

Bounds, E. M.: *Power Through Prayer* (Lubbock, Texas: Missionary Crusader, Inc., n.d.).

Grubb, Norman: *Continuous Revival* (Ft. Washington, Penn.: Christian Literature Crusade, 1961).

Grubb, Norman: *The Liberating Secret* (Ft. Washington, Penn.: Christian Literature Crusade, 1955).

Grubb, Norman: *The Spontaneous You* (Ft. Washington, Penn.: Christian Literature Crusade, 1970).

Hession, Roy: *Be Filled Now* (Ft. Washington, Penn.: Christian Literature Crusade, 1968).

Stanford, Miles J.: *The Green Letters.* Available from Christian Correspondence, Box 7507, Colorado Springs, Colorado 80907.

Taylor, Jack R.: *The Key to Triumphant Living* (Nashville: Broadman Press, 1971). A book destined to be a classic on the Spirit-filled life.

Tryon, David: *But How* (Chicago: Moody Press). The "how" of the Spirit-filled life.

Unger, Merrill F.: *The Baptizing Work of the Holy Spirit* (Wheaton Ill.: Van Kampen Press, 1953).

II. Outreach Ministries

Beal, Bohlen, & Randabaugh: *Leadership and Dynamic Group Action* (Ames, Iowa: Iowa State University Press). One of the best books available on small groups.

Campus Crusade for Christ materials, Arrowhead Springs, San Bernardino, California 92404. Thoroughly tested, well-developed. Write for samples of everything!

Christensen, Winnie: *Caught with My Hands Full* (Wheaton, Ill.: Harold Shaw Publishers). How one woman saw her neighborhood. "Must" reading for TOUCH leaders.

Christensen, Winnie: *Caught with My Mouth Open* (Wheaton, Ill.: Harold Shaw Publishers, 1969). Tremendous report of how one woman's Neighborhood Bible Study took off like a jet.

Faith at Word Editors: *Groups That Work* (New York: Faith At Work Press). Many other excellent materials on the small group which can be adapted for evangelism are available from this source.

Kunz & Schell: *Examine the Record* (Dobbs Ferry, New York: Neighborhood Bible Studies). Neighborhood Bible Study guide on Mark.

Kunz & Schell: *How to Start a Neighborhood Bible Study* (Dobbs Ferry, New York: Neighborhood Bible Studies).

Kunz & Schell: *The Acts of the Apostles: 18 Discussions for Group Bible Study* (Dobbs Ferry, New York: Neighborhood Bible Studies).

Neighbour, Ralph W., Jr. *Witness, Take the Stand!*. Available from Evangelism Division, Baptist General Convention of Texas, 306 Baptist Building, Dallas, Texas 75201.

III. On Understanding People's Needs

Berne, Eric: *Games People Play* (Grove Press, 1964). Astonishing insights into the psychology of human relationships.

Fromme, Alan: *The Ability to Love* (Pocket Books, 1966). Excellent, Mature insights; chapter on "Love and Friendship" especially good.

Hart, Juanita: *Brick by Brick*. Available from Evangelism Research Foundation, 14827 Broadgreen, Houston, Texas 77024. Late 1972 publication date. Excellent study of spiritual-psychological problems of the Outsider.

Jabay, Earl: *Search for Identity* (Grand Rapids: Zondervan Publishing House). A "must" book for those preparing to initiate work with Outsiders.

Tournier, Paul: *The Healing of Persons* (New York: Harper & Row, 1965). Insights into finding "the hole in the heart."

IV. Useful Tools for Outreach

Christians, Cliff, Editor: *The Way*. Monthly magazine for use in cultivative evangelism. Order sample from Laymen's League, Box 6191, Grand Rapids, Michigan 49506.

Coleman, Robert, *Established by the Word of God* (Huntingdon Valley, Penn.: Christian Outreach). Bible lessons for new Christians.

Coleman, Robert: *The Spirit and the Word* (Huntingdon Valley, Penn.: Christian Outreach). Bible lessons for Spirit-filled Christians.

Lewis, C. S.: *Mere Christianity* (Macmillan Press, 1943). Excellent background for the presentation of Christ to Atheists.

Rinker, Rosalind: *Teaching Conversational Prayer* (Waco, Texas: Word, Inc., 1970). Well-written book on how to use this powerful method of group praying.

V. General

Bender, Urie: *The Witness* (Scottsdale, Penn.: Herald Press, 1965). Best book in print on basic philosophy of witnessing.

Bennett, Thomas R.: *The Leader and the Process of Change* (New York: Association Press). Insights into waking changes without conflict.

Burdick, Donald W. *Tongues: To Speak or Not To Speak* (Chicago: Moody Press, 1969). A sane discussion which discourages glossolalia.

Haney, David P.: *Renew My Church* (Grand Rapids: Zondervan Publishing House, 1971). Designed for retreat use by adults who need to get into Outreach ministries.

Morris, George: *Imperatives for Evangelism* (Nashville: General Board of Evangelism of the Methodist Church, 1967).

Murray, Ian H.: *The Forgotten Spurgeon* (London: The Banner of Truth Trust, 1966). A side of Spurgeon that every pastor needs to see.

Neighbour, Ralph W., Jr.: *The Seven Last Words of the Church* (Grand Rapids: Zondervan Publishing House, 1972 publication date).

Packer, J. I.: *Evangelism and the Sovereignty of God* (Downers Grove, Ill.: Inter-Varsity Press).

Reid, Clyde: *Groups Alive—Church Alive* (New York: Harper and Row, 1969).

Rinker, Rosalind: *The Open Heart* (Grand Rapids: Zondervan Publishing House). Step-by-step portrayal of what the Christian experience is all about.

Watson, G. D. "Others May, You Cannot" (Westchester, Ill.: Good News Publishers). A tract which has meant much to the author.